Sesame and Lilies Paraphrased

John Ruskin's Classic in Modern English by
Leslie Noelani Laurio

Copyright © 2017 Leslie Noelani Laurio

All rights reserved.

ISBN: 1546458999
ISBN-13: 978-1546458999

CONTENTS

1. Sesame: Of King's Treasuries . . . pg 1
2. Lilies: Of Queen's Gardens . . . pg 21
3. Preface to Later Editions . . . pg 44
4. The Mystery of Life and its Arts . . . pg 57

1 SESAME: OF KING'S TREASURIES

Before I begin, I'd like to apologize for the vague title of this essay. I'm not going to talk about kings, nor about their vast treasures. I'm going to talk about another kind of royalty and another kind of riches than we usually think of. I want to talk about the treasures hidden in *books*, and tell you how we can find them--and how we can lose them. That's a serious subject, and a wide one! In fact, it's so wide, I could never even attempt to exhaust it. All I hope to do is to bring up a few simple thoughts about reading that seem more impressive to me every day as I see public opinion wanting to expand education. The way to do this is to read more.

Because of my connection with education, I get letters from parents about their children's education. What strikes me about most of these letters is how often the idea of 'a position in life' seems to be the prevailing concern to the parent. They're always asking about getting ahead, this always seems to be the thought in their mind. These parents never seem to be seeking an education simply for the good of learning, or even for the training and discipline it can bring. Instead, all they seem to care about is an education that will ensure a lucrative career, that will enable their child to rub shoulders with the upper class, that will earn him enough money to buy a home in a well-to-do neighborhood, to get ahead in life--this is all they hope for. It never seems to occur to them that there might be such thing as an education that will result in real life. Anything less is no kind of living, but merely existing. This kind of essential education is easier to have than they imagine if it's approached the right way, but no amount of money can buy it if it's approached in the wrong way.

First of all, we should ask ourselves: what does it really mean to 'get ahead' in life? For many people, it means being noticed and admired. It means being in a position that gains the respect or honor of others. It's not so much having money as it is being known in circles of well-to-do people. It's not so much doing some wonderful deed as it is being thought of as a wonderful person. In other words, it's about praise and admiration. That desire for public approval is the last weakness of noble minds, but it's also the first craving of weak minds, and the strongest impulse of average minds. The greatest things attempted by people are often traced to a desire for praise, while the worst things are often the result of a desire for pleasure.

I don't intend to criticize or extol this craving for praise. I just want to show how it's at the root of all effort, especially in our modern era. Stroking our vanity seems to be what motivates us to work, and what pleases us when we reflect on our lives. A seaman doesn't usually strive to be promoted to Captain because he thinks nobody else can manage the ship better than he can. No, he wants the promotion so he can be *called* Captain. A lawyer doesn't strive to be a judge because he thinks nobody can mete out justice more fairly than he can; no, he wants the position so he can be called 'your Honor.' And a congressman doesn't aspire to the presidency because he believes nobody else is able to run the country as well as he can. He wants everybody to call him Mr. President.

This is our idea of getting ahead. We want to work our way up to the higher classes, not because the people there are any better, but because it reflects better on us to be there. If that circle of people wasn't well-known for being exclusive, we would have little interest in being accepted into it.

When they stop to think about it, most people believe that doing one's duty is a high motive, although maybe not as important as earning a place of position or office. Being of use or doing real good is also usually high on our list of motives. Honest men don't deny that having a position of power or high visibility provides unique opportunities to accomplish good. And most people would agree that it's better to associate with sensible, well-informed people than ignorant fools, no matter whose company you're seen in public with. Our real happiness and opportunity for doing good depends on choosing true friends and wise companions.

And yet, even if we know this, and even if we have the presence of mind to choose wisely, the selection of people we have to choose from is limited to the sphere of people in our acquaintance. Almost everyone we know is determined by chance or necessity, and restricted to a narrow circle. It's impossible to know everyone we'd like to, and even those we do know aren't always around when we want to talk to them. The smartest people in the world aren't accessible to just any common person. We might be lucky enough to spot some great composer walking down the street, or meet a wonderful author at a book-signing, or raise our hand and ask a question at a physics lecture. We might even get to shake a congressman's hand and have a few words with him, or catch the eye of a member of the royal family. We covet these brief connections with great people and go through a lot of effort trying to see these people, and yet there's a group of great people who will meet with us any time we want, and will talk to us as long as we want, no matter who we are or what our station in life. Not only will they spend time talking to us, but they'll take the time to choose the best words they can find, and they'll share what's most important to them. Some of these people are rulers, and politicians, and thinkers. They're patient enough to linger around waiting for us in our libraries and on our bookshelves--yet we neglect their company, and sometimes don't care to hear a word they have to say for days on end.

You might say that you prefer living people whose faces you can see, because you can actually be right there in their presence, and that's more important than the words they say. But is that really true? Suppose you were able to go into a room where Abraham Lincoln or some wise sage was sitting behind a curtain and you had the chance to hear him but not see him because he was hidden behind the curtain--would you say 'no thanks,' or would you jump at the chance to just hear what he had to say? What if he was doing more than chatting casually, what if if he had thought out something very important that he wanted you to know, and he had searched his mind for the best words and the most concise phrasing, would you want to hear him although you couldn't go beyond the curtain? Would you want to know what he had to say? What if that curtain was made of paper, and was bound within the covers of a book? We have this opportunity, yet we often don't care to hear what's between the pages of a book.

You might say that living people are more interesting because they talk about what's going on right now. But that can't be the whole story, because even they will save the best of what they have to say for writing, and their casual talk will be about trivial, less urgent matters. But even when we do read, we often prefer reading light, trendy publications that are soon outdated rather than stiff, enduring classics that deserve to be called books. Did you know that there are books for today, and books for all time? I'm not just talking about quality. It's not as simple as saying a bad book doesn't last and a good one does. There are good books for all time, but there are also good books just for today. There are also bad books for all time, and bad books for today.

A good book for today is one that's useful or pleasant to read from a person you can't sit with over a cup of coffee and chat with--it's what they would say to you if they could, neatly printed and packaged in the form of a book. It might have useful information about health or starting a website. It might be as pleasant as a friend's chat, telling about a visit to a middle-eastern country, or explaining a political issue in accessible language, or telling a human interest story. All of these are books for today--useful and/or enjoyable now, but outdated in ten years. In our Information Age, there's no shortage of these kinds of books. We should make use of them, and be ashamed of ourselves if we don't take advantage of what they have to offer. But we should not allow them to monopolize our time so that we don't have time to read the more worthy *timeless* books. After all, those aren't books in the same sense as classics are. They're more closely related to newspapers and magazines. A friend's email or blog post might be delightful or even newsworthy today, but is it worth printing for re-reading next year? The newspaper is fine for catching up on events, but it's hardly the mind-broadening kind of reading you'd want to study. Even if you print off a friend's Facebook posts and get it bound in book form, it's not a real book you can read and re-read to learn from. A real book is more than communication or information. It's something permanent. A mere publication is just a way for someone with something to say to say it to a wider audience since it's logistically impossible for him to reach a lot of people in person. The publication multiplies his voice, but what he has to say is relevant only today. That is different than a book for all time.

But a book--a real book--is not just written to multiply a person's voice, but to store it for future generations. The author has something to say that he feels is true and useful, or helpful and beautiful. As far as he knows, no one has ever said it before, and there isn't anyone else to say it. He feels he *must* say it, and as clearly and beautifully as he can--especially, he must say it clearly. Of all he has in his life, he feels like this is the one thing he knows and has. This is the one bit of real knowledge, or lucid truth that his experience and understanding has allowed him to own, and he feels compelled to write it down for posterity, or engrave it in stone, as if to say, 'This is the best part of me. Everything else in my life was mundane--I ate, I drank, I slept and loved like everyone else. My life was as fleeting as vapor before I died, but I saw and knew this one thing. If anything in my life is worth remembering, this is it.' And *that* is what he writes down. In his own small way, and with whatever inspiration or gift he might have had, that is what he leaves behind. And *that* is a real Book.

Do you doubt that these kinds of books have ever been written? Do you doubt in honesty or kindness? Do you doubt that a wise person could have honesty or goodness? I hope you're not that cynical! The fact is, whatever part of a wise man's work is done honestly or out of goodness is his life's art--his book. It will always be mixed with fragments that aren't so worthy--parts that are clumsily worded, or repetitive, or artificial. But if you read thoughtfully, you'll be able to tell which are the true parts. Those are the parts that are truly the Book.

Books like this have been written in all times by the era's greatest men-- by a society's greatest readers, greatest politicians, and great thinkers. These are all at your disposal to choose from, but life is short. If you invest time reading one thing, then you won't have that time to read something else. If you waste time reading something trivial today, you can't get that time back tomorrow. Why should you spend time gossiping with the grocer or your barber, when you could be sharing the important thoughts of kings and philosophers? Why should you strive to get the attention of common people you meet all the time, and listen to their tidbits of news and chatter when the eternal court is open to you with all of its great people from all different times and different places, all kinds of writers, the most select, and the most noble? You can enter that society any time you want, you can decide which of them to hang out with according to your own whim. They will never turn you away. The strength of their character will test your own character, and your reasons for wanting to be part of that society will be revealed, whether your motives are true and sincere.

It isn't just a matter of wanting to be part of that society; you have to make yourself fit for it. The only way into this society of authors is by effort and worthiness, there is no other entrance. It can't be bribed with money, or awed by a famous name, or deceived by fancy clothing. No vile or vulgar person can get in. The guard at the gate only asks one question: do you deserve to enter? Then you may go in. Do you want to be friends with noble, worthy people? Then make yourself noble and worthy, and you will be. Do you want to hear what wise people have to say? Then learn to understand their words. There is no other way. You must aspire to their level, because they will not lower themselves to yours. A real, living politician might make an extra effort to be polite to you, and a living thinker might work hard to dumb down his words so you can understand them, but this society of deceased authors will not put on company manners or interpret their words for you. You will have to rse to the level of ther thoughts if you want to be delighted by them. You'll have to learn to share their feelings if you want to recognize their presence.

That's what it takes. I admit, it's no easy task. You have to learn to love those people if you want to be among them. Ambition isn't enough. They have no respect for mere ambition. You must really love them, and show that love in two ways.

First, you must really want to be taught by them and understand their thoughts. Notice that I said you have to understand their thoughts, not find your own thoughts expressed in their words. If the writer isn't any wiser than you, then there's no point in reading it. If he is wiser than you, then he'll think differently than you in many ways.

And, second, rather than thinking, 'what a great book! That's exactly what I think!' We should be thinking, 'How strange! I never thought of it that way before, yet now I see clearly that he's right! Or, if I don't quite see it now, I hope I will some day.' The point is, you need to read to get at the author's meaning, not to find yours. Feel free to draw conclusions if you think you're qualified, but first be sure you understand what he's saying. If a writer is worth anything, you won't be able to grasp everything he says at first. It will probably be a long time before you truly understand it. It's not that he isn't saying what he means, and saying it passionately, but he can't say it all. And he'll use parables and hide the meaning to be sure you're sincere about wanting to understand. I don't know why wise men tend to hide their deepest thoughts. It's as if they offer it as a reward to make you work for it, and they want to make sure you really deserve it before they allow you to understand. It's the same way with gold. We don't know why gold isn't waiting in heaps at the tops of hills so that people can get it whenever they want it without the trouble of locating it, digging it up, melting it down, and making coins out of it. But that's not the way it is. Nature hides it in cracks and it takes a lot of digging (sometimes unsuccessfully) to get it.

It's the same with great men's wisdom. When you open a good book, you have to ask yourself, 'Am I willing to work at mining for the truth in this book? Are my tools ready? Am I rested and in the right frame of mind to get to work?' Think of the author's meaning as the gold, his words like the rock that has to be chipped and melted to find the gold. Your own effort is like the pickaxe, and your own thoughtful soul is like the furnace that melts and purifies the gold. It will take your sharpest tools and most patient grinding to gather even a single grain of gold.

The first task is getting into the habit of looking carefully at individual words and being sure of their meaning. This has to be done syllable by syllable, or even letter by letter. This is why the study of books is called 'literature,' and why a scholar is called a man of letters rather than a man of books. A person could skim all the books in a city library and still be more illiterate than a person who studies ten pages of a single good book letter by letter--in other words, with real accuracy. This accuracy is what makes the difference between an educated person and a functionally illiterate one. *[More pages follow about accuracy in language and word study, particularly in English, where so many words have been borrowed from other languages. A word translated inconsistently can give different shades of meaning than the author may not have intended. He gives examples, such as translating the same word in our Bibles as pastor in some places in the text, and bishop in others.]*

Examining an author word for word helps us to understand exactly what he meant, rather than seeing it through the filter of our own personality and assuming he meant something else. This is how we can be sure we understand 'what Milton thought,' and not misread his thoughts. As you do this more and more, you'll think less about your own thoughts. You'll begin to realize that what *you* thought isn't very important. In fact, your thoughts and opinions might not have been the wisest and clearest that a person could have on the subject. Even more, unless you're a uniquely extraordinary person, you haven't ever really had any original 'thoughts' about important matters at all. So, rather than trying to figure out what you think, you'll invest more time and effort finding out the truth. The only real opinions you probably have are those concerning your personal duties--how you do your job, or how you run your household. It's common sense to have those kinds of opinions. We are also obligated to have true opinions about what's right and wrong: it's wrong to lie and steal, and God expects us to be hard-working, kind and honest. But when it comes to more complicated subjects, like doctrine, politics, science and art, we know almost nothing, and therefore we aren't qualified to make judgments. The best thing to do, even for a well-educated person, is to be silent, listen, try to learn more every day by making an effort to understand the thoughts of others. As you make an honest effort to understand, you'll begin to see that the thoughts of even the wisest people are often only pertinent questions. What they really do is define the issue clearly and show that there are so many angles to any issue that it's difficult to come to a conclusion. Besides clarifying the issues for us, they do us a real service if they can poetically 'mix music with our thoughts and sadden us with heavenly doubts' at the same time. The best writers are such broad-minded thinkers that you can't always pin down what they think about things. By comparing their writings, could you tell what Shakespeare's and Dante's opinions were on church authority? Both of them knew men and understood them very well. They both wrote about man's struggle between his flesh and his soul in heaven. They must have had an opinion, but it's not so easy to tell what it was.

It will probably take a long time before you really grasp the true meaning and purpose of these great writers, but even a little bit of sincere study will help you see that what you thought was your own opinion was really nothing more than incidental prejudice and vague stray thoughts that happened to drift your way. As a matter of fact, most people's minds are not much better than wild stubbly wasteland--neglected, mostly barren, and overgrown with pesky weeds. The best thing to do is to set fire to this wasteland, so to speak. Burn away the scrubby brush and weeds, plow up the clods of dirt, and sow fresh seeds. In order to do the work of digging for 'gold' in books, you must first 'break up your fallow ground and sow not among thorns.'

II. Once you have listened faithfully to these great teachers in order to understand their thoughts, there's one more thing you have to do. You have to enter into their hearts. Once you've begun to listen to their clear vision, you need to stay on course until you finally share their great passion. Yes, their passion. The word is nothing to be afraid of, nor is the thing itself. Some people speak against passion and feeling, as if we need less of it, but I think we need *more* of it, not less. The thing that sets a man apart and makes him noble is just this: he feels more than other people. If we were sponges, it might not be important for us to feel. If we were earthworms who could be cut in half with a shovel at any moment, it might be better *not* to feel anything. But we are human, and it's good for us to feel. In fact, we're only as human as we are sensitive, and we only have as much honor as we have passion.

Remember when I said that no vile or vulgar person could enter the society of great writers? What exactly is a vulgar person? It's a person who lacks feelings. Simple vulgarity is a lack of training that makes a person dense, but true deep-rooted vulgarity consists of a terrible callousness. In its worst extreme, it makes a person capable of all kinds of animal behavior and crimes with no fear, no pleasure, no horror, and no pity. Callous vulgarity is the result of a person's fist clenched to hit, a dead heart, filthy habits, and hardened conscience. The more a person is incapable of feeling sympathy, the more he's trapped in vulgarity. It is impossible for a such a person to have quick understanding, or tact, or the kind of compassion that mothers embody. This sort of sympathy should guide our Reason, and sanctify it. Reason can only determine what is true; it's the compassion of humanity that can recognise the things that God made that are good.

And now we come to the society of dead writers. We don't just want to learn from what's true; even more, we want to feel what's just and right. In order to feel along with them, we have to become like them, and that will take some effort. True knowledge is tried and tested knowledge, it's not simply the first thought that comes into our heads. In the same way, true passion is also tried and tested, and not just the first feeling that comes along. The first passions that come along are vain, false, and deceptive. If you yield to them, they will carry you wildly far, far away, chasing the wind in empty zeal, until your purpose and passion are gone. There is no such thing as a feeling that's wrong in itself, but any feeling can be wrong when it isn't disciplined and controlled. The nobility of a feeling is in its durability and fairness. A feeling is wrong when it's weak and wasted on trivial causes. There's a kind of idle sense of wonder, like a child feels when he sees someone juggling golden balls. That is a simple and basic feeling. There is nothing base about wonder itself, and it's this same wonder that makes us feel a sense of awe when we see God 'juggling' the golden balls of stars in the heavens. There is a basic level of curiosity that a child has when he opens a forbidden door, or eavesdrops into someone else's conversation (nosiness!), but there's a noble curiosity, too. The noble kind of curiosity is what makes a person face danger to see where a great river begins, or what's across the oceans. There's an even more noble kind of curiosity that causes us to ask Who made the river, and what's beyond the heavens. There's a basic kind of anxiety that we feel when we watch some disaster in a suspense movie, but it's right to feel some anxiety about the fate of a nation in the news. The tragedy is that our country wastes its passions on narrow, selfish matters. We squander our feelings on pretty things and speeches, parties and pleasure trips, sporting events and movies. Meanwhile, we are unmoved by nations where real people are being murdered daily.

I said that such passions are 'narrow' and 'selfish,' but I could have just as accurately said 'unjust' and 'unrighteous.' A gentleman is distinguished from a vulgar man because his feelings are unvarying and fair, and a result of deliberate reflection. These are the same things that distinguish a gentle nation from a brute mob. A mob can be whipped into a frenzy over anything. A mob might have fairly generous and good feelings as a general rule, but it has no deliberate foundation for these feelings. So, it can be swayed or worked up to anything on anyone's whim. A mob 'catches' opinions like people catch a cold. There's nothing too trivial to get a mob worked up about once it's been excited, and nothing so important that it won't go on its way and forget all about it an hour later, when the frenzy is over. But a gentleman, or a gentle nation, has passions that are fair, consistent, and constant. A great nation doesn't focus all of its attention on considering the evidence of a single thug who committed a murder. It doesn't turn a blind eye to thousands of people killing each other in its streets, and only show concern for what the effects might be on the price of electronics with no thought for who's right and who's wrong in all this killing. A great nation doesn't send a homeless man to jail for stealing a loaf of bread, and allow its investors to steal hundreds of thousands of dollars with impunity, or allow a bank that made its millions investing many blue-collar workers' life savings to close its doors because of 'circumstances beyond its control.' It doesn't allow companies that have gotten rich from plundering foreign countries' assets and drug money to buy up huge plots of land. A great nation doesn't allow its citizens to risk their health and shorten their lives so that slumlords can make a few extra dollars from them every month--and then have emotional debates about the heartlessness of not saving the lives of murderers on death row. A truly great nation can find the most humane method for ridding the country of murderers, and yet be able to distinguish between a planned murder carried out in cold blood, and one done in the heat of anger. A great nation doesn't act like a pack of angry wolves when some young guy goes crazy and commits a murder, or a gray old man has a fit of insanity and kills someone, while sending a diplomat to make polite speeches to a foreign ruler who regularly commits butchery of his own people. And, last of all, a great nation doesn't pretend to honor and reverence God while showing by its decisions and actions that it really cares only about money.

Why are we talking about reading, anyway? A country in a state like ours can't possibly read. It can't understand even a sentence from a great writer. In our greed and baseness, we are incapable of understanding any thoughtful writing. Fortunately, our nation's inner nature isn't yet corrupt. We still show compassion when something rings true. Although we're so infected with the idea that everything should pay that we hesitate to even play the Good Samaritan, yet there's still some capacity for noble passion in our collective thought. We show it in our work, and in our wars. We show it in private injustices that make us seethe with anger--although we can overlook a public offense in order to be polite. We work busily and industriously until late into the night, although our goal is money. We are willing to brave in battle and even give our lives, although we rarely stop to ask ourselves what we're fighting for and whether the war is justified. We're loyal to our own loved ones and will die for them, although even animals do that.

As long as these things are true, a nation still has hope. As long as it is ready to give its life for its honor (even if it is a silly kind of honor), or for its love (even if it is a selfish love), or its business (even if it's not a very worthy business), there is still hope for it. But it's only a hope. Its instinctive, reckless generosity can't last. No matter how generous a nation may be, once it has become like a mob, it can't last. It needs to direct and discipline its feeling, or else its feelings will direct it and discipline it--to its regret. Most of all, a nation can't last once it becomes a money-making mob. It cannot exist if it continues to despise literature, science, art, nature and compassion because its soul is focused on profit. Do think my words are harsh or exaggerated? I'll prove it to you, point by point.

1. We, as a nation, have despised literature. What do we care about books? Compare what we spend on our public and private libraries as compared to what we spend on our cars. If a man spends a fortune on his library, we think he's eccentric and call him a bibliomaniac. But when a man puts his money into his race cars, we don't call him a caromaniac, even though men are ruined every day from car races. Have you ever heard of men being ruined from their libraries? Or, would all the books in all the libraries in the country sell for as much as all the wine in the nation's wine cellars? What if you compared how much we spend per year on books vs. what we spend per year on eating out? We sometimes say books are like food for the mind. A really good book contains an inexhaustible amount of mind food, but how many people would pay as much for a book that will nourish their mind and enhance their life as they would pay for a good fish dinner? In the past, some men went

hungry and stinted on clothing to buy a book. I'll bet their entire library didn't cost as much as most men pay for one night's dinner. Few of us have to make that kind of sacrifice for a book. It's too bad, because a precious thing is more valuable to us if we've had to earn it or make sacrifices for it. If books were to cost even half as much as expensive dinners, or a tenth of the price of a gold bracelet, even fools might begin to wonder if there might be some value in reading as well as eating out and wearing jewelry. But books are so cheap that even wise people forget that any book worth reading is worth buying. If a book isn't worth enough to pay money for, then it can't be worthwhile to read, either. And a book isn't really useful until it is used: read, re-read, loved, underlined and marked in the margins so you can find your favorite parts as easily as a soldier can find his weapon, or a cook can find his essential spices. Plain bread is good, but there's one kind of bread that's as sweet as honey, if only we would eat it. That bread is found between the covers of a good book. A family would have to be pretty poor not to be able to afford some books when they provide so much for us. We think of ourselves as a rich nation, yet we're so cheap that we won't spend money on our own books. Instead, we borrow them from libraries because that's free.

2. We, as a nation, have despised science. I know what you're thinking. 'But aren't we ahead of everyone else in making discoveries, and aren't we thrilling the whole world with our inventions?' Yes, that's true, but that's all privately funded work, not something the nation itself supports. In fact, that sort of scientific work is done *in spite* of the nation, with the enthusiasm and funding of private citizens. Sure, we're happy to put new discoveries and inventions to profitable use. When there's money in it, we're all over it, but when someone asks us for financial backing for scientific research, that's a different story. What have we, as a nation, done to promote science? We need to know there's a storm coming to protect our ships, so we pay for an observatory. We allow our legislators to grudgingly give some support to our museums (the Smithsonian), assuming it to be a good place to keep stuffed birds and to amuse school children. If someone is willing to pay for their own telescope and make some discovery of a nebula, we're as proud as if that was our own discovery. If one of our sportsmen accidentally realizes that the earth has more to offer than a place to ride dirt bikes, and then finds gold or coal buried underground, we see the usefulness of his discovery and shower him with honors. But why should we take any credit for what *he* discovered?

Here is an example that illustrate our attitude towards science. A couple of years ago, some rare fossils were going to be sold in Bavaria that contained a unique specimen of a previously unknown species. It was expected to fetch $29,100 and was offered to our country for $16,200, but we wouldn't even give that! It would have ended up in some museum in Russia if Professor Owen hadn't taken time and effort to convince the public to persuade the government to pay $9700 for it, and he made up the difference! The public will pay him back eventually, but grudgingly, because they don't really care about the whole matter, and they never will unless some tangible (profitable) good comes from it, and then we'll take credit for it. Consider that we spend 75 million dollars for public expenditure, and a third of that goes to the military. It's like a wealthy man who spent $48,500 annually for his gardener and gated driveway, and claimed to be a science buff, and was approached by his servant about a unique collection of fossils on sale for &1.78. After keeping the servant waiting for a few months, it's as if he said, 'I'll give $1.13 for them if you'll loan me the remaining sixty-five cents until next year.'

3. We, as a nation, have despised Art. But, you say, don't we have extensive art exhibitions, and pay tens of thousands of dollars for a single painting, and have more art schools than any other country on earth? Well, yes--but that's all business. You'd sell coals as happily as canvas, and plastic pipes as happily as paintbrushes--whatever makes a buck. You'd take every other country's food if you could. You're not able to, so you stand like a troll at the bridge, calling out, 'Whaddya need? I'll sell it to you.' You have no clue; you imagine it's easy to have paintings like the beautiful French pictures of sun-browned vines and the Italian pictures of volcanic cliffs. You think that art can be learned like accounting, and when it's learned, it will give you more account books to keep. But you don't care any more about beautiful paintings than you do about the receipts and bills in your cold, dead office cubicles. You have no clue which paintings are in the museums of your country, whether they're good ones or not, and whether they're being maintained properly. When you visit foreign countries, it doesn't bother you in the least to see the noblest paintings the world has ever known rotting in some abandoned wreck of a building. If you heard that all the fine pictures in Europe were being ground into sandbags to bolster an Austrian fort, it wouldn't interest you as much as that weekend's football scores. And *that* is your national 'love' of art.

4. We, as a nation, have despised Nature. I'm talking about the profound, sacred sensations of beautiful natural scenery. Like the French

revolutionaries who used holy cathedrals for horse stables, you've made race courses out of Nature's cathedrals of the Earth. Your idea of fun is to tear around Cathedral Earth's carpeted aisles on your dirt bikes, and eat off its sacred altars. You've built ugly railroad bridges over beautiful waterfalls, and destroyed the shores of lovely lakes. There is no quiet valley where you haven't built a smoky factory, or mountain you haven't sliced open to mine for minerals. You've even gone to colorful foreign cities and cluttered their picturesque streets with ugly hotels and souvenir shops. Even the most beautiful serene snow-capped mountains are nothing but ski-slopes for you to slide down, shrieking at the tops of your voices. Two of the saddest sights I've ever seen are our tourists in the valleys of the Alps, amusing themselves by firing off old shotguns, and Swiss winemakers celebrating the harvest by using the vineyards for target practice. It's a sad thing to have only the dimmest notion of one's duty; it's even more pathetic if this is one's idea of fun.

5. Last of all, we, as a nation, have despised Compassion. I don't need to say much to prove this; I just need to show you a newspaper article:

An inquiry was held concerning the death of Michael Collins, 58 years old. Mary Collins, a miserable-looking woman, said she lived with the dead man and his son in a room on Cobb's Court. The man had been a boot-mender. He and his son would buy old boots, mend them as good as new, and re-sell them to shoe stores for whatever they could get, which wasn't much. The dead man and his son worked night and day to pay for the room and buy a little food to keep the family together. On Friday night last week, the man got up from his cobbler's bench and began to shiver. He threw down the boots he had been working on and said, 'Somebody else will have to finish these when I'm gone; I can't do any more.' He said he'd feel better if he was warmer, but there was no fire. Mary Collins took two pairs of mended boots to the shop to sell, but she could only get $12 because the shopkeeper said, 'We have to make some profit, after all.' She bought a few pounds of coal and a little bread and tea. Her son worked all night trying to mend boots to earn more money, but the man died the next morning. The family had never had enough to eat. The coroner asked Mary Collins, 'Why didn't you go to the workhouse?' She said, 'We wanted to stay together in the comfort of our own home.' A juror asked, 'But what comforts did you have? All you had was a dirty bed in the corner; even the windows were broken.' Mary Collins began to cry and said they had had a quilt and a few other little things. Her husband had always said he would never go to the workhouse. In the summer, when there was more work, he could make as much as $40 a week. They would save as much as they could for the next week, which would often be bad. In winter, they wouldn't even make half that much. For three years, things had been going from bad to worse. The son said he'd been helping his father for twenty years. They had often worked so late into the night that both he and his father had nearly lost their eyesight. The son currently has a film over his eyes. Five years ago, the dead man had gone to the church for aid. The church gave him a 4-pound loaf of bread and told him not to come back looking for handouts. That disgusted the dead man, and he would never go back. Things continued to get worse and worse until last Friday, when they didn't even have a few cents for a candle. The dead man lay down on the bed and said he didn't think he'd live till morning. One of the jurors told the son, 'You yourself are dying of starvation. Go to the workhouse just until summer!' The son said, 'if I did that, I would die. When I came out again, I'd have to start my business from scratch. No one would know us, and we wouldn't even have our rented room. I'm sure I could work now if I just had some food, because my eyesight would improve.' The medical records stated that the dead man had collapsed from weakness; he was exhausted from lack of food. He had no sheets or blankets. For four months, he had eaten nothing but bread. There wasn't even a particle of fat on his body. There was no sign of disease. If he had had some medical help, he might have survived. The medical record officially stated, 'The deceased died from exhaustion brought on by lack of food and basic necessities of life; also from lack of medical attention.'

But why wouldn't the man just go to the workhouse? Oddly enough, poor people seem to have a prejudice against the workhouse that rich people (who don't have to work there!) don't seem to have. Anyone who gets a pension from the government might be said to be in a workhouse. But the 'workhouse' for the rich doesn't involve work. It's more like a playhouse than a workhouse. The poor seem to prefer to die independently. Maybe if we made *their* workhouses as pleasant as the playhouses of the rich, or sent their pensions to their homes instead of making them go to the workhouse for them, or allowed them to 'misappropriate' money like the rich do, then maybe they'd be reconciled to the workhouse. But the truth is, we make our charity so insulting to them, or so uncomfortable, that they'd rather die than accept our help. Or else we leave them so untaught and ignorant that they can never get ahead, and they starve like animals, not knowing the right questions to ask, or where to go to help themselves. So I am right that you despise Compassion. If you didn't, that news story could not have happened in a Christian country like ours. Did I say Christian? If we were an UNChristian country, it would have been impossible for such a story to have happened. It's our imaginary Christianity that allows such things to happen. We wallow and bask in our faith for the pure emotion of it, romanticizing it like we do with everything else imaginary. We love the drama of the organ and the altar call, the sunrise service, the revival tent. We love toying with religion in stories about Satan, such as Faust, (or The Devil and Daniel Webster?). We chant hymns in front of stained glass windows for effect, sway and sing repetitive praise songs with feeling, and pass out tracts to convict the heathen multitudes. We pride ourselves on our holiness, and have nothing to do with those who disagree with us. But to put our faith into action and do a good deed? It would be more possible to get lightning from our incense smoke than to get real action or passion from our modern religion. Get rid of your incense, your organ, your stained glass windows. Give them to the city. Give it all up, and go take care of the poor man begging on your doorstep. Because wherever one hand reaches out to another to offer help, that's where the true church is.

As a nation, we have despised all five of these virtues. There are a few individuals who are the exception, and you benefit from their effort and passion and life. If not for them, your wealth, amusement and pride would be impossible. But you don't even thank them. In fact, you have no use for them, or forget them. The policeman risks his life patrolling to keep your stuff safe, and you never thank him. The sailor wrestles with the stormy sea, the researcher pores over his books and experiments. The common worker does his duty without thanks, and often at minimum wage, to keep your way of life uninterrupted. These are the people who make the country run, but they are not the country. They are only the body and muscles, acting on instinct, but the mind is gone. The only thing we care about is being entertained. Our religion is more performance and preaching to keep the mobs contentedly working while we amuse ourselves. We are becoming addicted to amusement. Our nation's moral state is diseased.

When people are thinking properly, enjoyment grows out of their work like colorful petals grow out of a flower. When people are compassionate and helping others, their emotions become consistent, deep, enduring and give life to the soul like blood pulsing through the body. But we currently have no real business of our own, so we spend our time on the delusive business of making money. We have no real emotions, so we have to stimulate our feelings with guilty pleasures. We don't execute justice in the real world, so we write about it in plays. We destroy the beauty of nature, so we enjoy enjoy the beauty of shows. The valid grief we should have shown for our fellow man is spent on tragedies in novels.

We can't know what the cost of all this is. We unwittingly cause (or fail to stop) thousands of deaths every day, but we don't mean any harm. We are the cause of oppression and destruction of peasants' property, but we would be sorry to find out we had harmed anyone. We are still kind-hearted, and still capable of virtue, but only on the surface, like children are. Thomas Chalmers, after a long life, said, 'The public is just a great baby!' What does any of this have to do with reading? Our national faults and miseries stem from illiterateness and lack of training in basic thought habits. Our problem isn't evil, or selfishness, or stupidity. It's the kind of reckless thoughtlessness of a schoolboy, except that a school boy has more hope because he at least recognizes that he has a teacher in authority over him.

There's an interesting illustration of us in a painting of Turner's. It's a drawing of the churchyard in Kirkby Lonsdale. You can see its lovely brook, the valley, the hills, and the misty morning sky. And oblivious to all this beauty, and in disrespect for the dead who are buried there, a group of schoolboys have piled their schoolbooks on top of one of the tombs and are throwing stones to try to knock the books off the grave! In the same way, we toy with the dead who could teach us; we push them away from us by neglecting the words they've left us. The pages of their books don't just lead to their gravestones; they lead to the gate of a great city full of sleeping kings. They would wake up and talk to us if we knew how to call them by their names. So often, even if we do enter through the gate, we wander around those sleeping kings, touching their robes and feeling the crowns on their heads, but they don't tell us anything. They seem like old, dusty antiques because we don't know the magic spell that would wake them up. If they heard that spell, they would immediately wake up and greet us, squinting thoughtfully and considering us. Instead of saying, like the fallen kings in Hades would say to newly deceased kings, 'Have you become weak as we are, and come to join us?' They would say, 'Have you become as pure and noble-hearted as we are, and come to join us?'

Magnanimous means having a mighty heart and a mighty mind. A person who is magnanimous is great in life. To grow closer to magnanimity is what real 'getting ahead in life' means. There's an ancient Scythian custom when the head of a household would die. They would dress the dead man in his best clothes, put him in his chariot, and have him carried around to his friends' houses. At each house, they would place the dead body at the head of the table and have a feast with him. What if you could be on the receiving end of this honor? Imagine that your spirit were slowly dying every day, your flesh growing cold, your heartbeat slowing down--but you'd be dressed gaily and driven around in a golden chariot, medals pinned on you, a crown put on your head. People would bow in front of your cold body, stare at it, follow it through the streets, build mansions for it, feast with it. You'd have just enough presence of mind to be aware of what was going on, and feel the crown and clothing, and see all your friends feasting around you. Would you choose this? Would any of us want to go through that? And yet, this is not so different from the way many of us live. Everyone who wants to get ahead in life by collecting cars, servants, money, and public honor, but doesn't seek real life, is choosing such an existence. The person who is truly experiencing real life is the one whose heart is getting kinder, whose passions are getting warmer, whose mind is getting quicker, and whose spirit is finding God's peace. Those who have this kind of life are the *real* kings and queens. The others are merely dressing and playing the part.

I am sometimes amazed to hear people talk about kings and rulers as if nations were a personal possession that could be bought and sold, as if countries could be acquired like sheep for eating or stripping of their wool. That mindset makes out kings and rulers to be like people-eaters, and makes it sound as if a king's dominion can be added to as easily as enlarging a man's private homestead. But kings who think like this aren't real kings any more than a horse-fly can be king of a horse. The horse-fly might bite and annoy the horse, but it can't guide it. Misguided kings with all their counselors and armies are just an enormous swarm of horse-flies carrying bayonets instead of stingers, and blowing trumpets instead of buzzing. They might not be as ugly as horse-flies, but they're just as harmful. Real kings, the good kind, rule quietly if they rule at all, and they don't like to lead. In fact, they decline to lord it over their people. Those who do lord it over the people find that, as soon as the people are useful to the king's purposes, they refuse to be tyrannized over and rebel.

But any king might become a real one as soon as he learns to measure his dominion by its strength rather than its size. It doesn't matter how many horses or castles a king may have; what matters is whether his men do what he says. Do they come when he says, 'come,' and go when he says, 'go'? What matters is whether his people hate him and die by him, or love him and *live* by him. A good king measures his dominion by his subjects, not how many square miles his kingdom is.

And yet, a kingdom cannot be measured. Who can measure the difference between a king who works alongside his people and teaches them, and a king who consumes and destroys and is the undoing of his country? This kind of king has a power that's like moth-eaten cloth and rusted tools. The moth kings collect treasures for moths to eat. The rust kings who aren't any stronger for their people than a rusted shovel, collect treasures for rust to destroy. The robber kings hoard treasure for another robber to steal from him. Hardly any kings have hoarded the kind of treasure that doesn't need to be locked up and guarded--the kind of treasure, in fact, that we wish lots of thieves would want to take. Moth kings, rust kings and robber kings have collected clothing that gets ripped, weapons that decay, and jewels that are stolen. Imagine if there was another kind of king who read about a fourth kind of treasure that was more valuable than silver or gold. It might be as rare as cloth woven by Athena herself, or impenetrable armor forged by the god Vulcan, or the three gods of 'Right Conduct,' 'Work,' and 'Good Sense' offering to teach and guide. If there were kings who sought after treasures like that, they would gather treasures of Wisdom to share with their people.

Imagine how amazing that would be! How unbelievable, compared to the state our rulers and country are in now! Imagine training our people to read instead of to fight. Imagine a wisely led army trained and paid to think instead of trained to kill! Imagine a nation finding entertainment in libraries as well as on the shooting range. Or given prizes for defending a premise with facts as well as for hitting a range target. It seems absurd to imagine the wealth of capitalist economies supporting literature instead of war.

Allow me to share a paragraph of the only thing I've ever written that's worthy to be called a book. If anything of mine lives on, this will survive everything else I've written.

'It's a terrible fact about the way Europe's economy operates that it is always money from capitalists that funds unjust wars. Regular wars don't need so much financial support. Most men who are fighting for a just cause will fight for free. But in an unjust war, men's bodies and lives have to be purchased with money, as well as the weapons, tanks and bombs that make war so expensive. Unjust wars also have a cost in fear and suspicion between countries that aren't good enough or honest enough to use their resources to work for peace. France and England spend ten million pounds a year on their military. Modern war isn't paid for so much by pillaging the conquered enemy, but by taking out loans from capitalist countries, and then taxing the people, who have no choice in the matter, to pay it back. Thus, it's the will of the capitalists that are the biggest cause for war. At the root of war is the covetousness of the entire country, blinding it to faith, sincerity, or justice. And the result is that each person, in the end, has to pay a personal loss and suffer some kind of punishment.'

France and England are spending ten million pounds a year to purchase panic and terror. What if they decided to be at peace and used that money instead to educate their people, and fund libraries, art galleries, science museums, gardens, and parks? Wouldn't they both be better off?

It will be a long time before that ever happens. But I hope it won't be long before every city has a library with the same collection of books in each of them--carefully selected books, the best available in every subject, written especially for the purpose, published the same size in easy to read type on pleasantly colored pages that would be sturdy, easy to handle, and beautiful. These libraries would be open at all hours to anyone, and the only requirements would be that the libraries should be quiet, and patrons must keep the books clean and in good condition.

I could detail other plans for art galleries, science museums, and other valuable and necessary things, but this book library is the easiest and most necessary. It would provide a cure for what ails us--we seem sluggish. We have an unnatural thirst and an evil hunger; we need healthier mind food. You were successful at repealing the corn laws. How about establishing new 'corn laws,' laws that would mean a better kind of food than corn? I'm referring to the kind of mental mind food that's like bread made from the old Arabian grain, sesame, which magically opens doors. Only these aren't doors to robber's caves, but doors to King's Treasuries.

2 LILIES: OF QUEEN'S GARDENS

"Let the desert and dry region be happy; let the wilderness rejoice and bloom like a lily!" (Isaiah 35:1, New English Translation)

Since this essay is a sequel to to the Sesame essay, I should tell you my intention for both of them. The question I suggested in the first essay (how to read, and what to read) came out of a deeper question that I hoped you would ask yourselves, which is, *why* to read. I hope you agree with me that whatever advantages the availability of education and literature in our modern era provide can only be useful to us when we understand clearly what education's result is supposed to be, and what literature is supposed to teach. I want to impress upon you that well-planned moral teaching and carefully selected reading can lead us to have a power over others who are badly guided and don't read. Depending on how much power we have, that can truly be a kingly power, giving to those who possess it the most noble kingship that humans can know. Too many other kings, although they might have crowns and riches, are either illusions or tyrants. The illusionary ones may have all the royal garb, but no real power. The tyrants exert their own will rather than love and justice, like good kings should.

There is only one *real* kind of kingship. It's the one ordained kingship, eternal and pure, whether the ruler wears a crown or not. This kind of king is morally stronger, and more thoughtful than others, and can therefore guide and inspire others. This kind of king's majesty is as stable and immovable as a statue--it doesn't wobble, or lose its balance. It is established and enthroned on a firm foundation of eternal law that nothing can alter or overthrow.

Literature and education are only useful when they promote that kingly kind of power: kingly power that we exert over ourselves, and through our own self-control, to those around us. What does this kind of royal authority look like when it's exercised by women? After all, women have a calling to be queens over their households and everything else in their sphere. If women understood their influence and exercised it with grace, their areas would be transformed with such a sense of order and beauty that they would find themselves reigning over Queen's Gardens.

And this brings us to another question that has infinite importance.

We don't know what a woman's Queenly power should be until we figure out what a woman's ordinary power should be. We can't determine how to educate them to fulfill their duty until we know what their duty is. There are so many opinions and wild ideas about what a woman's duty is, and the answer has repercussions for the happiness of all society. There has never been agreement about women's virtues, intellect, and capabilities in a man's world. People talk about a woman's mission, and women's rights, as if their mission and rights were totally separate from a man's, and as if they were independent of each other. Even more mistaken is the idea that a woman is only a shadow and helper of her husband, a weak servant who is mindlessly obedient and who needs the superior strength and courage of a man to support her.

This is an idiotic concept of the woman who was created to be a man's helper. As if such a weak, mindless slave could be any help to anyone!

Let's try to get a clear, true and harmonious idea of what female thinking and virtue look like in authority and function, as compared to a man's, and how a proper perspective of their collaboration with each other helps and increases the capability, honor and authority of both of them.

As I wrote in my last essay, education should first of all enable us to perceive the opinions of the wisest and greatest men on all kinds of complex subjects. Using books properly means going to those wise authors for help. We should ask for their insight when we lack knowledge and clarity of thought, and they can lead us into more open-mindedness and purer ideas than we had. They can give us the timeless collected wisdom of previous generations in contrast with our own isolated and unstable opinions.

With that in mind, let's ask for insight about women's true dignity and how women help men from the greatest, wisest and most pure-hearted writers. We'll start with Shakespeare.

First of all, Shakespeare has no heroes, only heroines. None of his male heroes are without some kind of flaw, except possibly Henry V, who was exaggerated for the play. Even Valentine from The Two Gentlemen of Verona is flawed. In Shakespeare's best plays, there is no hero. Othello, who came closest, might have been heroic if he hadn't been so simple that every vile temptation roused him. Coriolanus, Caesar and Antony were strong but deficient, and fell because of their pride. Hamlet was lazy and too distractedly analytical. Romeo was impatient. The Merchant of Venice gave in too submissively to bad luck. Kent, from King Lear, had a noble heart, but was too rough and clumsy to be useful when he was really needed, so he became nothing but a servant. Orlando was also noble, but a hopeless victim of circumstances. It was Rosalind who followed, comforted and saved him. But almost every one of his plays has a matchless woman: a woman who is steadfast even when hope looks lost, and has unmovable purpose. Cordelia, Desdemona, Isabella, Hermione, Imogen, Queen Catherine, Perdita, Sylvia, Viola, Rosalind, Helena, and last, and perhaps loveliest, Virgilia, are all faultless, illustrating the highest heroic type of humanity.

Consider, next, that the tragedy in every play is always caused by a man's foolishness or fault. If there's any redemption at all, it always comes through the wisdom and virtue of a woman. King Lear's tragedy is due to his own lack of good sense, his childish vanity, and his failure to understand his daughters. His only loving daughter's goodness could have saved him from the other two, but he casts her away.

I don't need to remind you of the story of Othello, or of the one flaw in his strong love. He isn't even as perceptive as the second female character, Emilia, who dies reviling him for misguided error, saying, 'You murderous show-off! A fool like you doesn't know what to do with such a worthy wife!'

In Romeo and Juliet, the wife's brave plan is ruined by the impatient recklessness of Romeo. In Winter's Tale and Cymbeline, two royal families that were lost and in danger through the folly and stubbornness of the husbands are finally redeemed by the noble patience and wisdom of their wives. In Measure for Measure, the injustice of the judge and the cowardice of the brothers stand in bold contrast with the victorious truth and purity of a woman. In Coriolanus, a mother's advice would have saved her son if he had heeded it in time. His forgetfulness is his ruin. Her prayers are the only thing that save him from a life of regret, since he destroyed his country.

And how about Julia, who remained faithful even when her beloved was fickle, wicked and childish? Or Helena, who was faithful to a sulky youth who insulted her? Or patient Hero and passionate Beatrice? Or Portia, who may have been 'unlessoned' but was still calm and devoted, seeming like a gentle angel bringing courage and help by her very presence and defeating the ugliest sins by her precise and accurate thinking (which women aren't supposed to be capable of doing) among men who are helpless, blind and vindictive?

In fact, of all the leading ladies in Shakespeare's plays, only one is weak. That's Ophelia, and it's because she isn't there for him when he needs a guide most urgently that the tragedy happens. And the fact that Shakespeare's few evil leading women (Lady Macbeth, Regan and Goneril) are such an exception among women, they seem to be a terrible deviation from Nature's order. Their influence for evil seems to be in the same proportion as the abandoned good they were capable of.

Thus we see Shakespeare's testimony of the position and character of women. In his plays, they are wise counselors, always faithful, strong enough to sanctify even when they aren't strong enough to save.

Next, let's consider Sir Walter Scott. He doesn't have the understanding of the nature of mankind as Shakespeare, nor the understanding of the root causes of fate and the directions it travels, but he does provide a broad view how people think in modern society.

We won't bother with his romantic prose writing or early romantic poetry, even though it's pretty; it has no weight, but is only the idealtic ideas of a boy. His really worthy works are the ones studied from Scottish life. they bear a true witness, and in all of them, there are only three really heroic men: Dandi Dinmont (a border farmer), Rob Roy (a bucaneer) and Claverhouse (a soldier fighting for an unworthy cause). Their only heroism is their courage and faith mixed with a strong but misguided intellectual ability. Walter Scott's younger male characters are gentlemen with fortunes who only play at life, and it's only because of their fortune that they survive the trials they find themselves in, although they don't really conquer them. You don't see any of his young men with even a trace of disciplined character, consistency, sincere in a deliberate purpose, or dealing with a hostile form of evil, meeting challenge with a resolute but controlled will. But his women--Ellen Douglas, Flora MacIvor, Rose Bradwardine, Catherine Seyton, Diana Vernon, Lilias Redgauntlet, Alice Bridgeworth, Alice Lee and Jeanie Deans--have various kinds of grace, kindness, and brains. All of them have an infallible sense of dignity and justice, and a fearless and untiring self-sacrifice that could act instantly, even when the duty they saw before them was merely the *appearance* of duty. And, finally, they all have a patient, wise and very disciplined affection that does a lot more than protecting those it cares about from a passing mistake. It gradually shapes, inspires and lifts the characters of those unworthy men it loves until we're able to tolerate hearing about their success, even though the men can take no credit for it.

Thus, in all cases, it's the same with Scott as it is with Shakespeare: it's the woman who watches over, teaches and guides the young man. It's never the other way around.

Let's look just for a minute at an even more serious testimony-- that of the Greeks and Romans. You've heard about Dante's Divine Comedy, how it's a love poem to his deceased lady, a song of praise asking her to watch over his soul. She stoops to have compassion on him, but never to really love him. yet even her compassion saves him from destruction and hell. He is on his way to eternal despair (hell), and she comes down from heaven to help him. As he progresses upwards through Paradise, she is his teacher, interpreting the most difficult divine and human truths for him, and leading him with rebukes from one star to another. I won't insist that Dante's perspective is infallible. If I kept on and on proving my point, you'd think my ideas were just the wild fancies of my poetic nature. Instead, I'll read you a few verses (from Pisano, by Pannuccio dal Bagno, translated by Rossetti) where a knight of Pisa is carefully writing to his living lady (Una). What he says is typical of a noble-minded man of his era.

"Understand that there is a law which says that my love for you should be shown by serving and honoring you. So I do, and I am content to be your servant.

"I am quite happy since I decided to obey this law of serving your excellence, for you are like a flower of joy. Nothing could make me regret my decision.

"Every thought and sense I have dwells on you, since all virtues have spread from you in the same way water gushes from a fountain. Wisdom's best help and honor is within you, and within you each heavenly good lives individually, and the combination of these attributes makes you perfect.

"My lady, ever since I comprehended how wonderful you are, my life has been different, set apart in shining brightness and truth. Before then, I had groped among shadows in a dark place, where quite a long time would go by without my having done anything worthwhile. But now, my service is yours, and I am full of joy and peace. Ever since I have lived for your love, I have been transformed from a mere beast to a man."

You might assume that a Greek wouldn't have as high an opinion of women as the Christian knight did. I admit that his spiritual submission wasn't as absolute, but as far as their own personal character, I could have written extensively about the Greeks instead of Shakespeare, but I don't think you would have been able to follow as easily. I will mention Andromache, whose simple mother's and wife's heart are the epitome of human beauty and faith. There's also the wise wisdom of Cassandra, although it wasn't heeded. Nausica was happy and had a playful kindness and simple princess-like life. Penelope kept a calm watch on the sea, patiently waiting for her husband. Antigone, the daughter and sister, was patient, pious and hopelessly devoted. Iphigenia submitted herself, silent as a lamb, to being sacrificed. And Alectis made the resurrection clear to the souls of the Greeks when she returned from the grave after calmly passing through the bitterness of death to save her husband.

I could produce more witnesses like this if I had the time. I could tell how Chaucer wrote a Legend of Good Women, but no Legend of Good Men. I could tell how Spenser's fairy knights are sometimes deceived and even sometimes conquered, but the soul of Una is never darkened, and Britomart's spear is never broken. I could go all the way back into ancient mythology and tell you how the Egyptians, who were at the time the wisest of all nations (and whose Princess was chosen by God to raise Moses), depicted their Spirit of Wisdom as a woman holding a shuttle for weaving. That spirit was adopted by the Greeks and became the goddess Athena with the olive tree and shield, revered as a precious ideal in art, literature, and representations of national virtue.

But I won't take time to wander into this mythical region of so long ago.

Just note how many great poets and thinkers throughout history have confirmed this view by their writings. You can see how consistently people have viewed woman's worth from ancient times. Were all these (male) writers just having a little fun, making up a pretend but desirable representation of the relationship between men and women? Perhaps their illusion is even harmful, since this is the exact *opposite* of what we consider the proper ideal of a marriage. We say that a woman should never guide a man, nor even think for herself, because the man is supposed to be the ruler, since he's so much more superior in knowledge, judgment and authority.

We need to decide where we stand on this issue. Are all these great men wrong, or are we? Are Shakespeare, Scott, Dante and Homer just writing fantasy, or, even worse, filling our minds with unnatural (and ungodly) ideas that could bring anarchy into our homes and ruin all affections? If you can even imagine that to be the case, consider the evidence of the human heart. In all the Christian eras that were distinguished for their purity or progress, men have yielded in obedient devotion to the women they loved. Notice that I said *obedient* devotion, not just enthusiastic, or worshiping some imaginary ideal. I mean entirely subjected, receiving encouragement, praise, reward for toil, and even direction for what kind of work to do, from his beloved lady, no matter how young she was. That is a kind of chivalry that requires the young knight to be subject to the command, even the eccentric command, of his lady. That kind of chivalry insults and dishonors cruelty in war, injustice in peace, and shameful, corrupt family relationships. That kind of chivalry is responsible for sustaining faith, upholding law, and cherishing love. That kind of chivalry obeys the lady's command because the knight realizes that the first impulse of every noble, well-trained heart is this kind of blind service to his lady. Where there is no such true faith and captivity to a lady, there is all kinds of perverse and wicked passion. A man's strength and the perserverance of his purposes are sanctified in this delighted obedience to his single love. This kind of obedience would not be safe or honorable if it were subjected to someone unworthy, but a rightly trained knight could never love anyone if he couldn't trust her kind suggestions or obey her prayerful command.

I won't try to convince you any more about this, because I think you know instinctively that it's true. Surely you don't think that a knight having his armor buckled on by his lady's hand was merely a casual, flippant kind of custom. It's a symbol of an eternal truth: that the armor of the soul can't protect the heart unless a woman's hand has fortified it.

It's only when she doesn't bind it tightly enough that the man's honor fails. Listen to these lovely lines by poet Coventry Patmore; they should be required learning for all the women of England:

'How wasteful woman is! She could have set any price she chose on her sweet self, knowing that man would pay whatever she asked to have her. But she has cheapened paradise and given away her gift for nothing. Now the bread is spoiled and the wine is spilled; if it had been properly used, it would have turned brutes into men--and not just men, but *divine* men!' (from Angel in the House)

I think you'll agree with me as far as that when it comes to the relationship of a man and woman who are in love. But can this continue through their whole lives? We think this kind of intense devotion is appropriate between a man and his betrothed, but not a husband and wife. In other words, such reverence and fond commitment are understandable towards someone's whose affections are still uncertain, and whose character we haven't fully figured out. But once we've secured possession of the person's affections and we've seen enough of their character that we're no longer hesitant about trusting it with our happiness, we withdraw that affection! Don't you see how unreasonable and pathetic this is? Don't you see that marriage, if it's a *real* marriage, is merely what confirms a temporary promise into perpetual servitude and modifies impulsive love into eternal love?

But you might ask, how do you reconcile the wise, guiding of an inspiring lady with the submissive role of a wife? In this: guiding and inspiring is not a determining (leading?) function. Let me explain.

We are inexcusably foolish when we say that one gender is 'superior' to the other, as if they were two of the same things that could be compared. No, each of them has something that the other one does not have. Each of them completes the other and is, in turn, completed by the other. They aren't alike in anything, and the happiness and perfection of both of them depends on each of them asking and receiving from the other for what only the other can give.

Here is a short description of their different characters. The man's function is active, progressive and defender. He is the doer, the creator, the discoverer, the protector. His intellect is for speculating and inventing. His energy tends towards war (when justified) and conquest (when necessary). But the woman's function is not for ruling or for battle.

Her intellect is not for creating or inventing, but for tidying, arranging, and making decisions. She's able to see the quality of things, what their rights are, and where they belong. Her service is to praise. She doesn't compete, but she determines the reward of the competition. She is safe in her occupation and position, and protected from danger and temptation. But the man, going to work out in the world, encounters all kinds of dangers and temptations. That makes him susceptible to failure, offense and mistakes. He is often wounded, beaten down, misled, and prone to callousness. But he protects the woman from all of this. She rules his house and keep out danger and temptation, error and offense. This is the true nature of Home: it is a place of peace. It is a shelter from physical hurt, fear, doubt, and division. If it is not a place of peace, it is not a home. If the husband or wife allows anxieties from the outside world to enter, or unloved, unknown, contradictory or hostile people, then home is no longer a place of peace. It just becomes another part of the outside world that you've roofed over and heated. But when it's a sacred place, a pure tabernacle, a domestic temple guarded by the household gods (the husband and wife) who don't let anyone in unless they can receive them with love--then its roof and fire symbolize a nobler shade and light. They symbolize the shade of a rock in a weary land, and the light of a lighthouse in a stormy sea. And then it does justice to the name and praise of Home.

No matter where a true wife comes from, if she's a truly worthy wife, this kind of Home will always surround her. Even if the sky and stars are her only roof, and a camp-fire is her only heat, yet Home is wherever she is. If she's a truly noble woman, this Home will stretch far around her, and that kind of home is better than any house with wood floors, or marble counters. Her home sheds its quiet light far away for the benefit of others who would otherwise be homeless. I believe this to be a woman's true place and power. But in order to fulfill this, she must be beyond reproach. If whatever she rules is not right, then nothing is right. She must, then, be enduringly good and incorruptible. She must be instinctively wise, but not wise for the purpose of her own development; her wisdom must be for self-denial. She must not be wise to set herself above her husband, but so that she can be successful at his side. She must not be wise with a petty, cold and haughty pride, but with the passionate gentleness of an infinitely flexible and variable service that's useful at many different kinds of things. This is where a woman is justified in being changeable. 'La Donna e mobile' (woman is changeable), but not 'Qual pium' al vento' (like a feather in the wind, at the mercy of the elements). Not 'as variable as the shade made by a quivering aspen tree,' but as variable as light itself, with many beautiful spectrums that reflect all the different colors that fall on it, and exalts it.

I have shown you what a woman's place and power should be. Now we need to ask, What kind of education is going to prepare her for this?

If you agree with my assessment of her position and dignity, it won't be difficult to figure out what kind of education will train her for her position and raise her to her dignity.

The first thing we must do for her is to get her the physical exercise that will keep her fit and enhance her beauty. Her beauty will be refined with activity and delicate strength. She can't be too strong. But remember that physical freedom won't make her beautiful if she doesn't also have a free heart. I'm going to reference two passages from Wordsworth, a poet who writes with power and rightness. These passages describe and point to the source of the woman's beauty.

'She grew under sun and rain for three years, and then Nature said, A lovelier flower was never sown on earth before; I will claim this child for myself. She will be mine, and I will create a lady of my own.
To her I will be both law and impulse. The girl will feel a guiding power to kindle or restrain in rock, plain, earth, heaven, glade or bower.
The clouds will lend her their form, the willow tree will bend for her. She will notice grace even in the storm's movement as it molds her by silent sympathy.
And vital feelings of delight will raise her and make her tall. Her pure heart will grow larger. These are the kinds of thought I will give Lucy while she and I live together in this happy dell.'

Notice where it says *vital* feelings of delight. There's such a thing as deadly feelings of delight, but natural feelings of delight are vital and necessary to our very life.

And if they're going to be vital, these feelings will have to be delightful. You can't make a girl lovely unless you also make her happy. If even a single restraint is put on a good girl's natures, even one check on her instinctive affections or attempts at effort, it will show in her features. There will be a hardness that will take away some of the brightness of innocence in her eyes and some of the charm in her virtuous forehead.

That was the 'how.' This is the result, a perfect description of a woman's beauty from the same poet:

   'A facial expression in which sweet memories meet promises just as sweet.'

The perfect beauty of a woman's expression must be one of majestic peace founded on the memory of happy, useful years, full of sweet memories--joining with an innocence full of promise, looking forward to changes to come. It is modest, bright, hopeful about the potential the future brings and the blessings she'll bring to others. While that promise still holds hope, there is no old age.

So, you have to get her in physical shape first, and then, as she is fit enough, fill her mind and solidify it with the kinds of knowledge and thoughts that will confirm her instinctive sense of justice and refine her natural mindfulness of love.

She should have whatever knowledge will help her to understand the world's work [*the work the men do*] and even offer some help. And yet, this knowledge shouldn't be given to her as if she might actually need to be doing it herself, but more so she can sympathize and help make determinations [*when issues arise; help the men in her sphere to see sides of issues they may have missed, as Charlotte Mason said*]. It's not urgently important that she knows many foreign languages, but it is extremely important that she is capable of showing kindness to a foreigner, or detect sweetness when a foreigner speaks. It's not vital to her own value or dignity if she knows microbiology or astro-physics, but it's vitally important that she be trained in the habits of accurate thinking, and understand that God's natural laws are beautiful and unalterable. She should study one science far enough along to realize how deep and vast that field is [*enough to know that the world is more complex than she thinks!*] and have respect for the brave, wise men who, like children in perpetual wonder, pursue those complex fields of science. It's not important how many cities she can identify on a map, or how many names and dates she has memorized--the purpose of educating women isn't to turn them into dictionaries or encyclopedias. We educate women because it's imperative that she can enter with her whole being when she reads a history story, so that she can picture it in her imagination, and feel the pathetic circumstances and dramatic events with true compassion; often a historian's cerebral Reason makes him miss that part and remain detached. But a woman is able to discern the justice of divine reward, and glimpse through the darkness the fateful threads that connect deeds with punishment. And, most of all, she needs to learn not to limit her sympathy, but to extend it respectfully to those whose lives she touches who are making history right now, and to current disasters happening in the world. If she understood them enough to genuinely mourn over them, she would make sure they could never happen again. She should be aware of what effect it would have on her if she were the one going through tragic circumstances, even when she doesn't want to see them. She should have an accurate realization of the smallness of her life and her little world as compared to the world God lives in and loves. She needs to remember that her devoted thoughts and prayers should be fervent even though the circle of people she prays for is small. Her prayers for her child's fever or her husband's headache shouldn't be more keen than her prayers for the multitudes of the desolate and oppressed who have nobody to love them.

You've probably agreed with me so far. But you might not like the most urgent thing I'm going to say. There's one area of study that is dangerous for women. They need to be careful how they even approach it: Theology. It's odd that women, who are so modest that they doubt their own ability and hesitate to submerge themselves into the study of science where every step, like math, is tried and proven, will yet plunge head-first with no thought of incompetence, into this study where the greatest men have trembled, and the wisest men have erred. It's strange that they'll smugly and pridefully mix whatever evil or foolishness they have in themselves, whatever arrogance, irritability or ignorance with such a holy subject, making it one bitter concoction. It's strange how women who are Love made visible will be so quick to judge and condemn what they know nothing about before they think to go to God and pray about it. And it's even stranger that they would think that the Holy Spirit, the Comforter would guide them into habits of thinking that bring discomfort into their very Homes, and turn the beautiful 'household gods' of Christianity into ugly idols of their own making. They 'dress' these idols according to their whims, and their husbands turn away in grieved scorn, afraid to say anything for fear of being yelled at.

With the single exception of studying theology, I think a girl's education should be pretty much the same as a boy's--the same subjects, but with a different direction. No matter what her station in life, a woman should know about whatever her husband is likely to know, although in a different way. His mastery of the subject should be foundational and progressive [*starting with the basics and getting deeper and deeper into the subject*]. A girl's knowledge of the same subject should be more general and geared for practical daily use that will help her husband. I actually think it might be beneficial for men to learn things in the same general, practical way, and save deeper study for those subjects that will best prepare them to be of use to society [*specializing in his career?*] The gist of my thinking is that when a man learns a language or science, his knowledge should be deep and thorough. A woman only needs to know enough to share in discussions with her husband and his best friends intelligently.

But, whatever she learns, she should learn with exquisite accuracy. There is a big difference between definite, basic knowledge and shallow, superficial knowledge; a difference between a solid beginning, and an ineffective attempt at a brief overview. A woman will always be helpful to her husband by what she truly understands, no matter how little that might be; by what she only half-knows, or misunderstands, she will only tease him.

If there's any difference between a girl's education and a boy's education, it should be that the girl should start earlier. Her intellect matures faster and is ready for deeper serious subjects before most boys of the same age. And the other difference is that her literature selections should be less frivolous [*rather than light and fluffy 'because she's a girl'*]. Her literature should be carefully chosen to add patience and seriousness to her quick wit and naturally sentimental nature. Quality literature will keep her thoughts high and pure. I'm not going to make any specific suggestions, but be sure not let her inhale foolish romances as fast as she can check them in and out of the library.

Also watch that she doesn't read too many of the wrong kind of novels. We shouldn't dread just the impurity that might be in a book, but we also watch any books a girl gets too worked up over. Even the most poorly written romance isn't as horrendous as the more base forms of sentimental Christian literature. The worst romance isn't as corrupting as falsified history [*even when written to amplify the Christian side of history?*], misleading philosophy, or distorted [*partisan?*] political essays. But even the best romance becomes dangerous if it's so thrilling that it makes ordinary life seem dull, and creates an unhealthy desire to experience the kinds of dramas that don't happen in real life.

Thus, when I mention novels, I'm talking about quality novels. Our current [*Victorian*] era is unusually rich in these kinds of books. If these books are read well, these books can have a weighty use, since they're actually commentaries on human moral make-up and chemistry--studies of human nature. But they rarely serve this function because they're hardly ever read seriously enough to allow them to do this. The most they can usually accomplish is to increase the goodwill of a kindhearted reader, or else increase the bitterness of an ill-tempered reader, because every person gathers from a novel whatever mental food fits their disposition. From reading the books of Thackeray, those who are naturally proud and envious will learn to despise humanity. Those who are naturally gentle will learn to pity humanity, those who are naturally shallow will learn to laugh at humanity. Novels might have some use for us by bringing vividly to our attention a truth about humanity we had only vaguely conceived of before. But the temptation to over-write with flowery language is hard for even the best writers to resist, and it can turn people off to reading so that they've actually done more harm than good.

I'm not going to suggest how much novel reading should be allowed. But I will say this: whatever books are read, whether they're novels, poetry, history or whatever, they should be chosen because of the good qualities in them, not simply for a lack of impurity.

The possible incidences of less savory things in a powerful [*high quality, useful*] book won't do any harm to a great-hearted girl, but she will be oppressed if an author is hollow, and a book that treats foolishness in a breezy, lighthearted manner will degrade her. If she has a collection of old classics [*pre-Victorian*] available, then she can have full and free access to them with no concerns. But keep modern magazines and modern novels away from her. Instead, turn her loose among the old classics every rainy day and leave her alone. She'll find whatever she needs better than you can. The difference between a girl's and boy's character is that you can mold a young man as if you were chiseling rock or hammering bronze. But you can't hammer a girl into anything. She grows like a flower. Without sunshine, she withers. Without fresh air, she rots in the bud like a narcissus. If you let her fend for herself without giving her help when she needs it, she may fall in the dirt and defile herself. But she cannot be chained up. She needs to be free to choose her own way. In both her mind and body, she must always have 'her movements light and free at home, she should be able to go wherever she wants in pure and innocent freedom.' So, let her loose in the library [*of old classics*], like you would let a fawn loose in a field. A fawn can tell which weeds are poisonous a lot better than you can. It knows which ones are good, too. It will eat some bitter and prickly ones that are good for it, though you never would have thought of offering them.

When it comes to art, keep only the finest examples in front of her. When she tries her hand at creating, make sure she's accurate and thorough, so that she comprehends more than she actually produces. When I say the finest examples, I mean the truest, simplest and most useful. Notice those words: they'll be relevant for all of the arts. Look at how they work in the area of music, where you'd think they wouldn't apply: The truest music is music where the notes and tune closely and faithfully express [*and match*] the meaning of the lyrics or character or mood. The simplest music is music where the meaning and melody are expressed with the least and most necessary notes [*not a lot of extra notes*]. And the most useful music is music that takes the best words and makes them their most beautiful, enchanting them in our minds as each word is matched to its own glory of sound, and brings those words to our hearts right when we need them most.

A girl's education should be as serious as a boy's, not only in content and progess, but especially in the spirit. Don't raise a girl as if she were meant for nothing more significant than decorating a man's arm, and then complain about how superficial she is. Give her the same advantages you give her brothers. Appeal to the same noble instincts of virtue. Teach her as well as her brothers that courage and truth must be the pillars of her being. As brave and true as she is, she will respond. Yet most girls' schools, even in our Christian society, act as though the way a girl enters a room is more important than courage or sincerity. Our whole society displays cowardice and deception towards her. It displays cowardice when it doesn't dare to allow her to live or love in any way except that which is dictated to her, and it displays deceit when it parades the exaggerated glories of the world's vanity in front of her at the very time in her life when her entire future and happiness depends on her remaining undazzled and keeping her common sense.

Give girls not only noble lessons but noble teachers. You consider your options before you select a school for your sons. You consider the character of the principal. No matter what kind of man he is, you give him full authority over your son. You show him some respect: if he comes over for dinner, you don't make him eat in the kitchen. You know that at college, your son's teacher will be under the direction of the head of the department, and you have the utmost respect for him. You would never treat the Dean of Harvard as your inferior.

But what about when it comes to selecting teachers for your daughters? What kind of respect do you show them? Is a girl likely to take her own conduct or intellect seriously when you entrust the entire formation of her moral and intellectual character to a person you show less respect for than your housekeeper? Is your child's soul less important than your dusting and groceries? You act like you're bestowing some kind of honor on the woman by simply allowing her to sit in the drawing room in the evening!

There's one more area your daughter needs help with. This sometimes influences her more than anything else. She needs the help of Nature in all its wildness and freedom. Listen to this comment about Joan of Arc's education:

'The education of poor Joan was scanty, like everyone else's in her day, yet it was quite grand enough to meet a higher philosophical standard. The only reason that kind of education is not practical in our era is that we could never provide it.

'She owed a lot to the advantages of her situation, but she owed even more to her spiritual advantages. The fountain of Donremy was right next to a large forest. It was so haunted by fairies that the local priest had to read a mass there once a year to keep them in control.

'The forests of Donremy were the glory of the land. In them were mysterious powers and ancient secrets that dominated the people's minds. There were Abbeys with their windows 'like the Moorish temples of the Hindus' that held some power in Touraine and Germany's Diets [*diet: convocation or assembly*]. These Abbeys had lovely bells that were heard many miles away at prayer time. Each bell had its own story. These abbeys were few and scattered, so they didn't disturb the solitude of the area, yet there were enough of them to cover the area with Christian influence so that it wasn't a heathen wilderness.'

We don't live rural enough to have a forested area here as deep as 18 miles to the center, but we can have enough to keep a fairy or two for our children if we want to. Suppose you had a yard behind your house big enough for your children to play in, with just enough mowed area for the children to run, but no more, and you couldn't afford to move. Now suppose you could make a fortune by digging a mine right in the middle of your backyard and turning the flowerbeds into a coal mine. Would you do it? I hope not. You would be wrong if you did, no matter how large the fortune you could gain by it.

And yet this is what we're doing all over the UK. Our country is like a little garden with enough room for your children to run on the lawns if you let all of them run there. But we'd allow it to be turned into coal mines and filled with piles of ashes if we could, and it's the children, not us, who will suffer for it. The fairies won't vanish. There are coal fairies as well as fairies of the forest. Their first gift is angry 'sharp arrows of the mighty,' but their last gift is destructive 'coals of juniper.' [*Destroying the environment today will bring curses tomorrow.*]

Although I feel as strongly about this subject as I do about anything else, I can't pressure you. We appreciated the beauty of nature so little while we had it, that we'll never even know what we've lost. On the other side of the Mersey River is Snowdon, the highest mountain in Wales. The Menai Straits farther west, and its nearby granite rock beyond the moors of Anglesey which is beautiful when the heather is in bloom, was once considered a divine spot that looked westward. Holyhead is still amazing to see when the red light [*from the South Stack Lighthouse*] shines through a storm. There are hills and bays and blue inlets that the Greeks would have envied. Our Mt. Snowdon is like Greece's Mount Parnassus, but where are its muses? That mountain on Holyhead is like Greece's island of Aegina, but why don't we have a temple on it, like the Greeks have a temple to Minerva?

Shall I read you what the Christian Minerva accomplished under the shadow of our Parnassus before 1848? This is an account of a Welsh school in a town of 5000 people.

'Then I called up a larger class; most of them were new to the school. Three of the girls kept saying they had never heard of Jesus. Two said they had never heard of God. A third of them thought Jesus was still on earth' (not a bad thing, actually!) 'half knew nothing about the Crucifixion. Four out of every seven didn't know the names of the months or how many days are in a year. They had no concept of addition beyond two plus two or three plus three. Their minds were perfect blanks.'

Oh, women of England! From the princess of that backwards place to the simplest of you Englishwomen, don't deceive yourselves into thinking your own children can enter their place of rest while these ignorant people are scattered on the hills of Wales like sheep without a shepherd.

Don't imagine that your daughters can be trained to recognize the truth of their own beauty while the beautiful places God made for them to learn and play lie desolate and defiled. You can't properly baptize them in your churches' marble baptismal fonts without also baptizing them in the sweet waters that gush from the rocks of your native land--waters so pure that a pagan would have worshiped them. But you only worship them with pollution. You can't lead your children faithfully down to your beautifully carved wooden altars while the hazy mountain altars high in the heavens that sustain all of England are still uninscribed. Pagans would have seen the powers of heaven in every cloud from those mountain peaks. Those peaks are like altars built, not to an unknown God, but *by* the Unknown God.

III.

We've discussed the nature of women and a girl's education, her household responsibility, and her queenliness. Now we come to our widest question: what is her queenly duty regarding the community?

We generally think of a man's duties as public and a woman's as private. But this isn't totally true. A man has private duties relating to his own home, and public duties that expand from there to his community. A woman also has private duties relating to her own home and public duties that expand from there.

The man's private duty in his home is to maintain it, defend it, and see to its progress. The woman's duty is to ensure its order, comfort and beauty.

Think about what these tasks would look like if they were expanded. The man's duty as a member of the community is to maintain it, defend it, and see to its progress. The woman's duty as a member of the community is to assist in its order, comfort and beauty.

What the man does to defend his own home against insult and harm is the same as he does for his country, but in an even more devoted way. When his country is in danger, he leaves his home unprotected to do his obligatory duty to his country.

In a similar manner, what the woman does in her home, being the center of order, soothing pain, and reflecting beauty, is the same thing she does in her community, where order is more difficult, pain is more intense, and beauty more rare.

The human heart has an instinct that draws it to its intended duties--an instinct that can't be quenched, but can be warped and corrupted if you sway it from its destined purpose. This is no different from the instinct of love; love, when it's properly disciplined, preserves the hallowedness of life. But misgoverned love undermines the hallowedness of life. Love can only do one or the other of these. There's also the passion for power that manages all the greatness of law and life when it's used properly, but wrecks them when it's misapplied.

The desire for power is deeply rooted in the heart of both man and woman. God put it there, and intends for it to be there, so we shouldn't criticize the need for power. For the sake of God and man, we should desire it as much as we can. But what *kind* of power? That's the question. Do we want power to destroy, like a lion's claw and a dragon's fiery breath? That is wrong. Or do we want power to heal, redeem, guide and guard? The power of a royal scepter and shield, a royal hand with a healing touch that limits the enemy and frees the captive, a throne whose foundation is the rock of Justice, and can only be descended from by the steps of Mercy: this is the right kind of power and throne to crave. This kind of power makes women no longer simply housewives, but queens.

It's been a long time since women assumed a title that once only belonged to nobility. At one time they only accepted the simple title of 'gentlewoman' because it was the counterpart of 'gentleman,' but later they insisted on the title of 'Lady,' which corresponds to nothing less than the counterpart of 'Lord.'

I don't criticize them for this, but only for their short-sighted motive in this. It's a good thing for them to want and claim the title of Lady, as long as they want and claim the responsibility and duty that go along with it and not merely the title. Lady means 'bread giver,' and Lord means 'protector of Laws.' Both titles refer, not to laws and bread of the household, but the law and bread in the broader context of the multitude. A man who goes by 'Lord' only has a legal claim to that title when he maintains the justice of the Lord of lords. A lady only has a legal claim to her title when she offers a Lady's help to the imperfect representatives of her Master. Women once ministered to Jesus from what they had and were allowed to help Him in that way. And women today may claim that title when they are known, as Jesus was, for breaking bread.

This generous representative dominion and power of the House-Lord and

House-Lady is great and venerable, not because of the number of past kings and queens who have held the title in the past, but because of the number of the multitude influenced by it. When its authority is founded on duty and its ambition is founded on doing good, the multitudes worship it reverently. Of course every girl wants to be a noble lady with a retinue of servants. Indulge in that desire! You can't be too noble, or have too great a retinue. Just make sure your retinue is made up of people you serve and feed, rather than slaves who serve and feed you. And make sure that the multitude who obeys you is made up of people you have comforted, not oppressed--people you have helped out rather than led into captivity.

This is true of the dominion of the household as well as the dominion of royalty. If you accept the highest responsibilty, you can also claim the highest dignity. The title 'Rex et Regina' and 'Roi et Reine' [*King and Queen*] both mean 'Right-Doer.' They're different from a Lord and Lady because their authority is supreme. They don't just feed and clothe; they also guide and teach. And, whether consciously or not, you must be revered in many hearts. You can't put aside the crown. You must always be queens: queens to those who love you, queens to your husbands and children, queens of higher mysteries to the world beyond, which will bow down before the myrtle crown of praise and the pure scepter of womanhood. But, unfortunately, you are all too often idle and careless queens, grasping to be first in the most trivial things, while you ignore the important things. You leave anarchy and violence to do whatever they want in the world, so that they defy the power that comes from the Prince of Peace, so that the power to do good is betrayed by the wicked and forgotten by everyone else.

Notice the name 'Prince of Peace.' When kings, or even nobles and judges, rule in that name, they receive the power of it in the area where they rule on earth. There are no other rulers on earth besides them. If there is any other power, it's the power of MISrule. But those who rule by the grace of God are all princes and princesses of Peace. There are no wars in the world nor injustices that women are not answerable for--not because they started it, but because they could have stopped it. Men are prone to fight by nature. They'll fight for any cause, or, if there is no cause, they'll fight over nothing at all. Whatever suffering there is in the world, or injustice, or misery--the guilt lies with women. Men can bear the sight of such ugly things, but women shouldn't be able to bear it [*and should therefore have put an end to it.*] Men are able to trample over anything without sympathy when they're in the midst of a struggle, because men are weak when it comes to sympathy and small when it comes to hope. It is only women who can feel the depths of pain and envision the way for it to be healed. But instead of trying to bring healing, women turn away from it. They shut themselves up in their beautiful homes and lovely gardens. They're content to know that there's a whole world out there of secrets they dare not encroach, and suffering they dare not imagine.

This is what amazes me the most about humanity. I'm not surprised at any depths to which humanity can be degraded when it has been warped from its honor. I'm not surprised that a miser can die with his hands still clutching his gold. I'm not surprised when a sensualist lives as if he were already dead. I'm not surprised when a murderer kills a single victim in the darkness. I'm not even surprised when a band of men or a frenzied nation murders a multitude boastfully in broad daylight. I'm not shocked by the countless horrendous sins of priests and kings. But there is one thing that does surprise me: seeing a sweet and kindhearted woman with a child at her breast, and a power over her child and her husband that is stronger than the seas--in fact, a whole ocean of blessing that her husband would never part with for any amount of riches--and yet she abdicates this power to try and be better than her neighbor! I am shocked to see such a woman, with innocent feelings fresh in her mind, go into her garden and finger the delicate petals of flowers, with a contented smile because she's safe within the walls of her peaceful isolated home-- yet, all the while, she knows in her heart that there's a world on the other side of her fence with men torn up from agony, and beaten down by the unrelenting hardship of their lives.

Have you wondered what the symbolic meaning is in our custom of strewing flowers in front of those we think are most happy [*such as at weddings?*] Do you think we're just trying to deceive them into imagining that happiness will always fall like that, in showers of petals at their feet, that wherever they travel, their feet will tread on sweet-smelling flowers, and the rough ground will be smoothed for them with rose petals? If they believe that, life will cure them of it by giving them bitter herbs and sharp thorns to walk on, and if their path is smooth, it will be because it's covered with snow. But we don't intend them to believe that. The reason we throw flowers is to illustrate how a good woman's way is strewn with flowers because they rise up behind her steps, not in front of them. 'Her feet have touched bare meadows and left daisies blooming.'

Is that just a romantic lover's dream, pretend and fanciful? What if it's true? Maybe you think this is also a poet's illusion:

> 'Even the lovely, light harebell raised its head,
> Made buoyant by her graceful footsteps.'

It's not enough for a woman to refrain from destroying wherever she passes. She should also revive. The harebells should bloom, not droop, when she passes. Do you think I'm exaggerating? No, not a bit. I mean every word of what I say. I mean it calmly and with all my heart. You've heard people say that flowers only flourish in a garden where someone loves them. I know you'd like that to be true. You'd think it was a nice trick if you could bring a brighter bloom into your flowers just by looking at them kindly. You'd like it even more if your look had the power to cheer and guard--if you could remove the black blight, and scare away the caterpillars, bid the rain to fall on them in drought, and say to the wind, 'Come, you south wind, breath on my garden so that it may smell sweet.' Do you think this is a great thing? Wouldn't you think it was even a better thing if you could do this for fairer flowers than these? What if your look could bless flowers that would bless you back, and love you back? What if these flowers had thoughts like yours, and lives like yours, and after they were saved, were saved forever? Wouldn't that be a much better power? Far away, among the moorlands and the rocks, in the darkness of the terrible streets, these little flowers are lying, with their dainty leaves torn, and their stems broken. Won't you go to them and set them in place in their flower beds, and put a fence around them to block out the fierce wind? Morning follows morning for you, but not for them. For them, dawn rises to watch them die, but not to breath fresh life to them. Can you hear the dawn calling you through your window, as if you were Dante's Matilda standing on the edge of the River of Forgetfulness, picking flowers? It says,

> 'Come into the garden, Maud,
> Night, which is as black as a bat, is gone.
> The woodbine scent is sent through the air,
> And the smell of the roses is blown away.'

Will you go down among these needy flowers? They are sweet living people. Their new courage has sprung from the earth with the color of heaven still upon it. Their courage is starting up straight and tall as a church spire. Their purity has had all its dirt washed away, petal by petal, into a flower of promise. But they still turn to you for help: 'The larkspur listens, I hear! And the lily whispers, I wait!'

There are two lines I left out of the poem above:

'Come into the garden, Maud,
Night, which is as black as a bat, is gone.
Come into the garden, Maud,
I am here at the gate, and I am alone.'

Who do you think it is, waiting at the gate of this sweet garden, waiting for you? Do you remember, not Maud, but Mary Magdelene, who went to the garden early in the morning and found Someone waiting at the gate, and she thought it was the gardener? Have you found yourself searching for Him often, all through the night, but in vain? He is not at the gate of the old garden [*of Eden*] where angels guard the entrance with fiery swords. He is waiting at *this* garden, all the time. He is waiting to take your hand, to show you the fruit in the valley, to see whether the vine is flourishing, and the pomegranite has budded. There He will show you the little tendrils of the vine that His hand is guiding. You will see the pomegranite growing where He threw the seed. Even more, you will see the Angels who guard the garden, who wave the birds away with their angel wings so they won't eat the seeds on the path. They will call to each other, 'Catch the foxes for us--the little foxes that ruin the vineyards while they are in blossom.' You queens, listen! The foxes shall have holes, and the birds shall have nests among the hills and woods in your land. Shall the very stones cry out against you in your cities, saying that they were the only pillows where the Son of Man was able to lay His head?

3 PREFACE TO LATER EDITIONS

I'm fifty-one years old now and unlikely to change my mind at this point on any important issues (unless I grow senile!), so I'd like to revisit my writings and add what seems needed to whichever of my books might be useful to future generations. As I do this, I might leave out a lot, but I'm not going to attempt to revise what I've already written. A young man isn't going to write like an old man, and it would be a waste of time to try to recapture the way I spoke as a young man. I also want to say that I am not ashamed of anything I wrote before. Much of my writing was rapidly penned for temporary purposes, and although it's still as true as it ever was, it's no longer relevant. On the other hand, what I wrote about religion was meticulous and persuasive when compared to most religious writings, yet I was completely wrong. I had been brought up in a narrow denomination and that had clouded the way I read history.

I'm finding some things in my older books that are still of value, but when I find them in my earlier books, they're often blemished from pretentious language. I wrote that way partly because I thought I needed to in order to be a good writer, and partly (as seen in Vol 2 of my book 'Modern Painters') because I was trying to copy the older, better stye of English literature, especially imitating my favorite prose writer at the time, Richard Hooker.

When it comes to art, conduct, and non-religious morality, I not only still agree with what I've written, but I wish I could re-affirm the essense of what I wrote . . .

The first book that needs a new edition is Sesame and Lilies. I've removed the entire preface about the Alps to use somewhere else, and I'm adding a lecture I gave in Ireland (The Mystery of Life and its Arts) because it goes along with the other two essays. I'm glad this new edition will be the first of my reprinted works for many reasons, although now that I look back on the two essays (Sesame, Lilies) I'm painfully aware that I wasted a lot of good work on them. I put a lot of thought and emotion into them, but I was foolish to think that a short lecture could arouse people to convictions I had come to after years of intense consideration. What was meant to be delivered as a public lecture is going be less effective when read quietly to oneself later. But I'd only weaken the essays even more if I tried to re-work them into actual book-style writing from their lecture format. I couldn't have done so at the time because I had a habit of impatiently putting my thoughts into intense wording more fit for a rousing speech than a book. Therefore, I'm surprised, as I re-read this, to see that there's a lot here that seems accurately and energetically written, if you'll pardon my boasting. I haven't seen anything put as convincingly or even as clearly, yet I can still imagine a person reading it and laying it aside, unmoved and unguided to put any of it into any definite course of action.

So, here and now, I will attempt to say briefly and clearly what I want my readers to understand, and what I hoped (and still hope!) they would do. Maybe then my essays will have better results.

The first essay (Sesame) says that life is short, and there are very few quiet hours in a life. Therefore, we shouldn't waste time reading worthless books. In a civilized society, valuable books should be available to everyone, in a quality edition, for a reasonable price--never printed with small type, or on brittle paper, or in an ugly edition, to save money. None of us needs *many* books, and the few we need ought to be clearly printed on good paper and strongly bound. We may be a desolate, poverty-stricken nation, hardly able to keep ourselves going, but even so, no person would knowingly drink bad wine or eat bad meat. In the same way, no one should have to settle for hard-to-read or loosely-bound books. Not many people can be rich, yet any person who works honestly ought to be able to provide himself with decent shoes, a decent coat, serviceable brakes for his car, and a good, strong binding for his books. I would urge every young man to begin a book collection for his future household as soon as he can. By wise budgeting, he should be able to slowly acquire a set of functional, sturdy books he can use throughout his life. His little (but steadily growing) library should be the most decorative and well-studied part of his room. Every volume should have its own proper place, like a statue with its own niche in the wall. And one of the first and most enforced rules a child should learn is how to turn the pages of a book carefully without ripping or folding the corners.

That was what I wanted to impress when I wrote 'Sesame: Of King's Treasuries.' I wanted to show how precious books are and what good they can do. But the next two essays were written to hopefully make the youth of England aware of the purposes of the adult life they were entering into, and the nature of the world they would live in and conquer.

These two essays are fragmentary and not arranged very well, and they can't be any more condensed. But the gist and conclusion of them can be summed up in the last six paragraphs of 'The Mystery of Life and its Arts.' If you don't read anything else of this book, read that part over at least twice. Those paragraphs contain the best verbalization that I've ever put into words of what I intend to do myself, and what I'll beg anyone under my influence to do. The letters I wrote to the workmen of England at the beginning of this year were my attempt to get them on board, with the aid of whoever in the higher classes they can trust to help them. Besides those six paragraphs, keeping recent events in mind, read the fable on page 170, and then paragraphs 129-131. The famine in Orissa * was real; 500,000 people died there, in one of *our* British dominions, because of carelessness and thoughtlessness. Remember that well. It is the best possible illustration of the way modern political economy works in real life, and of how it creates a relationship between supply and demand.

[*Famine of Orissa: India, 1866: there was a drought on the eastern coast of India. Orissa was isolated and dependent on rice being shipped in. The Bengal government miscalculated, and by the time the need was noticed, it was monsoon season. The British Indian government imported 10,000 tons of rice, but by the time it got to Orissa, many had already died of starvation and cholera. Predicting a shortage of rice the following year, the government over-estimated and imported too much rice, paying four times the usual price. Only half of it was used. After two years, 4 or 5 million people had died and the Indian government had spent too much on rice.]

Then read the second essay (Lilies) and it should be clear to the end. Since that essay was written, questions have come up about the education and rights of women. These questions have troubled simple minds and excited restless minds. Sometimes I'm asked to give my opinion on this issue, and I imagine some of my younger female readers, after finishing the second essay, might want to know what I think they should do in the present circumstances. This is what I would say to any girl who had enough confidence in me to believe what I told her and do what I said.

First of all, keep in mind that no matter how much you know, or what advantages you possess, or how good you might be, you have not been singled out by God who made you, from all the other girls in the world, to be expressly informed about His own nature and character. You were not born in a single bright spot in the universe where an un-erring doctrine of religion could be clarified to you from your earliest years, and where everything you learned would be irrefutably true, and everything you were taught to do would be infallibly correct. Of all of the arrogant, foolish ideas that anyone could entertain, this is the proudest and most ludicrous: that you are such a darling of the heavens, and favorite of the fates, that you were born in the precise time and the exact place when and where pure divine truth had been separated from the errors of all the other nations, and your father had been divinely purposed to buy a house in the very neighborhood where the only chosen church is where that pure and final truth would be proclaimed. Don't even think it. It's not true. In fact, the opposite is true. It may be unpleasant for you to think of, but it's comforting to me--you, with all your lovely clothes, and charming looks, and kindly thoughts, and righteous intentions, are no more thought of or loved by God than any other foreign child in a third world country. In fact, of the two of you, you probably know less about God than she does. The main difference between you is that she thinks very little about God that is correct, and you think a lot about God that is wrong.

So then, this is the first thing to grasp: you aren't perfectly knowledgeable about the most perplexing of all subjects [*religion*], so you should behave modestly and appropriately--and be silent about it.

The second thing to keep in mind is that, no matter how good you are, you have faults. No matter how dense you are, you can find out what some of your faults are. No matter how minor your faults are, you need to make some effort--not too painful, but patient effort--to get rid of them. Trust me when I say that, no matter how many faults you find or imagine you have, only two are of any real consequence: idleness and cruelty. Maybe you're proud. Well, some good can come from pride, if it's not religious pride. Maybe you're vain. In fact, you probably are, but that only makes it more pleasant for those who enjoy praising you.

Maybe you're a little envious. That's hardly shocking; almost everyone else is, too. Maybe you're cynical. That's concerning, but it only means that, if I knew you, I'd probably only enjoy talking to you that much more. But, whatever else you might be, don't be useless, and don't be cruel. In 6,000 years of thinking about right and wrong, wise men have agreed on one point and confirmed it through experience: God dislikes idle and cruel people more than anyone else. His first command is, "Work while you have light," and His second is, "Be merciful because you have received mercy."

"Work while you have light." Work especially while you have the light of morning--in other words, your youth. Nothing surprises me more than how old people fail to tell young people how precious their youth is. Sometimes old people regret their earlier days, or forget them. They often foolishly criticize the young or, even more foolishly, indulge and spoil them, or, most foolishly of all, thwart and restrain them. But you hardly ever hear old people warn or caution them. So I am warning you: the happiness of your life, the power of your life, and your share and rank in heaven depend on the way you spend your days *now*. Not that these should be sad days. Not at all. After all, the first duty of young people is to be delighted, and to be delightful. But in the most profound sense, these should also be solemn days. There is no solemnity as deep to a thinking creature than the solemnity of dawn [*morning, youth*]. These days shouldn't just be solemn in the beautiful sense of fresh beginnings, but also in character and how they are spent. The word 'solemn' comes from the Latin word 'solennis,' which means a regular or yearly observance. Remember that every day of your youth is decisively establishing the habit and practice of your soul for good or for evil. What you do now will either set down pure habits of precious and beautiful doings, or will entrench deeper furrows for seeds of sorrow. Therefore, make sure that not a day passes in which you don't make yourself a better person in some way. In order to do that, find out what you are now. Don't think vaguely about it. Get a pen and paper and write down as accurate a description of yourself as you can. Put a date on it. If you're afraid to, find out why. Try to muster up the courage to look deeply into yourself. I realize that the mind is not as pleasant to look at as the face, and that's why we need to look at it even more. Keep two mirrors on your dresser, and dress your body and mind in front of both of them every morning. After you're dressed, go about your day without giving them a second thought. Your hair may get wind-blown and need brushing, and your temper and thoughts might get ruffled throughout the day and need some smoothing, but don't carry around a mental pocket-mirror. Just check your mental state every morning.

Write down, honestly, what you are--or, at least, what you think of yourself. Don't dwell on those inevitable minor faults I just mentioned. When you do what you have to do to live a right life, those things will take care of themselves. Try to determine as well as you can what you're good at and what you can be made into [*focus on your strengths and not your weaknesses?*]. You will discover that merely resolving not to be useless, and sincerely wanting to help other people, are the best and quickest ways to improve yourself. So, from the beginning, think of all your strengths as tools to help others. Read paragraphs 74, 75, 19, and 79 with careful attention, and you'll understand what I mean about languages and music. In music especially you'll find that being useful has a personal benefit because, no matter how limited your talent is, you have enough voice and ear to sustain a note of tolerable range in a group piece of music. That's the first thing you should do. Train your voice to be disciplined and clear. Think only of hitting the note accurately, never think of expression or what kind of effect it's having on those who may be listening. If there's anything in your soul worth expressing, it will come out in your singing. But there probably aren't very many real feelings in you that need to be expressed [*that would do the world good*], so the best for you to do is to make your voice a clear instrument that people can depend on to hit the right note. It's the same with drawing. As soon as you get down on paper a recognizable shape and get across its character to another viewer, or make it look clear and interesting to a child, you'll begin to enjoy art for its own sake. Then all of your mental habits and your memory will help you get more precise. But if you only make ornate sketches to show off and get you praise, or pretty ones for entertainment, drawing will not have much interest for you, and it won't teach you anything.

Besides this delicate work [*of singing and drawing?*], determine to do something useful in a practical sense every day. First, learn how to run a kitchen. Learn the good and bad qualities of different common foods, and the best and simplest ways to prepare them. When you have time, go and help a poor family. Show them how to cook economically so as to make the most out of little, and how to make budgeted food taste and look tempting. Encourage them to make the most of what they have by folding their cheap napkins nicely, and putting a flower or two on the table. If you manage to get a decent meal on their table and make it pretty with a clean tablecloth, you can ask permission to say a short prayer, but let your ministry [*evangelizing*] be limited to that for the moment.

Devote a certain part of every day, even if it's only a short time, to making sturdy, attractive clothes for the poor. Learn the practical qualities and uses of the most common fabrics, and make everything the best quality you can, regardless of cost. There are many reasons for this, too many to share here, but trust me, and don't stint on quality. If you can't get a good bargain on good quality fabric, buy the raw material and get some poor women to help you weave it into cloth that can be trusted. Then, every day, make some small article of clothing, sewn by your own hands, as sturdily as it can be stitched, and embroider something on it to make it pretty enough that anyone would be proud to wear it. Continue making clothing until you hear of some honest person who needs clothing, which may sadly happen too often. Even if you end up being deceived and find out that your hand-made clothes were sold at a second-hand shop, don't let that discourage you. Someone who needs them will buy them from there. That's no business of yours. Your concern is to have good, clean clothes at hand when you see a child who needs them. After you've done this for a little while, you'll begin to understand the meaning of at least one chapter in your Bible without a commentary or sermon: Proverbs 31.

In these ways, and any others you can find to be of service, you must try as hard as you can to be usefully employed for a good part of the day so that at the end of it, you can say as proudly as any peasant, that you have not 'eaten the bread of idleness.'

The second thing I said is that you must not be cruel. Maybe you think there's no chance of that, and I hope you would never be deliberately cruel or unkind to any creature. The problem is, unless you go out of your way to deliberately be kind to every creature, you'll often unwittingly end up being cruel to many. Cruel, partly through lack of imagination [*inability to put ourselves into someone else's shoes and really feel their suffering*], and, even more so in our day, through the subtle encouragement of selfishness taught by church doctrine that says that evil will be brought to a good end. Though meant to help us patiently bear trials rather than trying to escape difficult situations, in actual practice, this doctrine results in us being content to think about future glory when other people are going through difficult situations [*instead of trying to help them out of them*].

With our recently improved and more accurate teaching, I don't think people will continue to think they themselves will be saved out of any danger or distress while those around them aren't so blessed. But they might still not be moved to kind deeds, and may continue to believe that pain and suffering is something to be born with patience [*rather than something to change by helping others out of their suffering*]. Consider this: there are some degrees of pain, like there are degrees of wrong-doing, that are bearable and appear to be normal trials or even divine discipline. For example, your fingers tingle when you go outside on a freezing morning, but that only makes them feel that much warmer when you go back indoors. Or, your muscles are sore and tired after a good day's hard work, but that only makes your rest that much more pleasant. Or you have to wait for something you really want, and you get weary of waiting, but it only makes it more anticipated and appreciated when it finally comes. But you can't carry a trial past a certain point. If you stay out in the cold too long, your fingers will get frostbitten. If you work too hard for too long, you'll collapse from exhaustion and never be the same. If heart-sickness goes past a certain point, the heart loses hope and spark forever.

In this respect, evil means suffering past the point of no return. It means sorrow or sin that ends in death. As far as we know, there are many kinds of pain and sin that can't have any other ending. Of course, we, being blind and ignorant creatures, can't know what seeds of good might be hidden in some present suffering or sin, but we can't worry ourselves with what we can't know. It's possible that murderers and liars might, in some distant and future universe, be exalted to a higher kind of being than they could have reached if they hadn't killed or lied. But our actions shouldn't be guided on that kind of speculation. I admit that a beggar in misery on our doorstep will find comfort in heaven, but Jesus, whose words are our only guide, never inflicted disease as a blessing, or sent the hungry away unfed, or sent away the wounded unhealed.

The only reliable thing to do is to define good and evil by our common sense, and try to promote good, and conquer evil as hard as if there were no other world than this one. Most importantly, get rid of the absurd notion that Heaven will interfere to correct major problems, but won't interfere in small ones. If you prepare a meal carelessly, you can't expect God to miraculously make it palatable. If you spend years on foolishness and ruin your life, you can't expect Divine interference to jump in at the last minute and make everything work out anyway. The world was not made that way. The consequences of big mistakes are as certain as the consequences of small ones. The happiness of your entire life and the lives that lie in your control depend on your common sense and judgment as surely as does the success of a well-planned dinner party.

Think carefully and honestly about these things, and you'll agree that they're true. And once you realize that, consider your position in life. I assume you belong to the middle or upper class, and that you'd be disinclined to descend into a lower sphere. You might like to think otherwise, and some strong-hearted and romantic few truly might not mind, but it's not wrong to not want to give up your sphere. Thus, I assume you have good food, nice rooms to live in, fashionable clothes to wear, the ability to have every reasonable and healthy pleasure you want. You're probably content and grateful for these blessings and thank God every day for these things. But why do you thank Him? Is it because you think that you are so blessed because you're a special favorite of God's? Is the essential meaning of your thanksgiving prayers, "Lord, I thank You that I'm not like other girls; not because I fast twice a week while they feast, but because I feast seven times a week while they fast"? Do you think this kind of prayer pleases God? What if you saw one of your real-life sisters thrown out of your family's home, starving, helpless, heartbroken. Would you go into your father's room and say, "Dad, you're so good to give me what you won't give my sister"? Whatever anger made him throw your sister out, do you think he'd be pleased with that kind of thanksgiving, or flattered by that kind of praise? Are you even so sure that he favors you over your sister? What if, all this time, he loves your sister as much as you, and he's only testing you, to see how you respond to her suffering? He might not be angry with her any more, but more angry with you, all the more for your 'thanksgivings.' It might be wise for you to sincerely consider your position, especially if you believe the scripture that says, 'How hard it is for rich people to enter the kingdom of God.' I doubt you believe it now; if you did, you wouldn't be so complacent in your state. You can't really believe it until you know what the Kingdom of God means. 'For the kingdom of God is not a matter of eating and drinking, but of righteousness, peace and joy in the Holy Spirit.' [*Rom 14:17*] This joy doesn't only come from going to church and singing praise songs. It can be joy in a dance, or in a joke, or something you've earned, or that you've given willingly. But there is no joy in anything that separates you from your fellow man, as if God specially favoring you, or that makes you look better because of their misfortune, or exempts you from the kind of work they have to do, or allows you to indulge while they're in distress.

Consider these things, and I think you'll start to feel--not a morbid kind of pity that will turn you into a somber Sister of Charity [*nuns who volunteer service dressed in black*], but a steady flame of continuing kindness that will make you a cheerful helper. I don't mean any disrespect to them. I know how good they are and how much we owe them, but professional devoutness is the wrong kind of spirit (except in cases where an organization is necessary to get the job done). In practice, they're merely like band aids applied to sores caused by diseases that never should have been allowed to exist in the first place. They encourage less worthy women to continue their frivolous lives by making them take an all or nothing view--if they can't be saintly enough to dedicate their life to charity, then they aren't good for anything. If you feel you must wear a uniform, then wear one--but let it be a pleasant and attractive one. And be a Sister of Charity in your heart, without requiring a veil or vow of obligation to confirm it.

I have one or two more points that are hard to write about, but this letter to the editor from The Times says it beautifully, so I'll include it:

Dear Sir--they say one example is better than many sermons. I have an example that's painful but I can't help dwelling on it.

France's crisis of ruin, humiliation and misery is the fault of French society and its recent luxurious habits, expensive clothes, indulgence in every kind of wasteful pastime. Our society is an example to England of what NOT to do.

Many French women must have bitter feelings of regret now that their days of luxury and wealth are over, and their bills of bygone splendor lie heavy on their consciences and wallets.

The evil affected all classes of society, high and low, as the examples of the wealthiest ladies were followed all too successfully by everyone else. Every year, dresses were more extravagant, entertainment was more costly, all kinds of expenses increased. The morals of society, its decency and manners degraded lower and lower. Magazines told all the scandalous gossip about celebrities--their parties, at clubs, attending movie premiers, outdoing each other in fashion, their latest romances and quotes. Living beyond one's means became a way of life as everyone tried to keep up with, or out-do, everyone else.

The result of all of this is our ruined prosperity and the downfall of everything that seemed bright and hopeful,

Sesame and Lilies

I am sad and afraid at my country's plight and suffering. I can't help but feel sorrowful when I see England following in our footsteps. Makeup and fancy hair, slang and vulgar movies, knowing fashion designers by name, and reading immoral books, are all small offenses in themselves, although a few years ago they would have been considered pretty bad. Yet they're a slippery slope that can tempt one all too quickly to take an even more dangerous road.

I wish all Englishwomen knew how much they're admired by other countries. Foreigners have a high opinion of their principles, their truthfulness, the fresh and pure innocence of their daughters, and their healthy young children.

Listen to what happened to me. During the days of the uprisings of 1848, the mob searched all the houses in Paris for firearms. The house I lived in didn't have any, and the man of the house kept saying there were none there. The furious revolutionaries were about to resort to violence when his wife, an English lady, bravely came forward and assured them that there were no arms hidden there. The mob immediately responded, 'You're English; we believe you. The English always tell the truth.'

I hope no one will think I'm unjustly critical, loving and admiring England as I do, if I see some alarming trends that concern me in England.

I have nothing against anything that can make life lovely and pleasant. I like to see a woman nice, elegant and looking her best in as pretty a dress as she can afford, or a healthy young girl riding her horse, or houses decorated as nicely as possible. But it can go too far--it's the degree beyond that which has ruined us. I hope our example will serve as a warning to you, and repay you for your help and friendliness to us in our days of trouble.

May the women of England accept this in the kind spirit of a New Year's wish from
    --A French Lady, Dec. 29

This is what I would say if I could say it convincingly to all of you, my young friends.

For older readers, I need to say something about what right I have to write about these things. Too much of what I've said has only been said in faith [*rather than from first hand experience?*] One wise, lovely lady told me when these essays first came out that she was sure 'Sesame' would be useful, but that I knew nothing about 'Lilies.' That was partly true. It was also more personal than some of my other writings because I wrote it to please one girl. If it wasn't for what I remembered of her, I might rewrite a few sentences of 'Lilies' in a different tone. As the years have gone by, I have had the opportunity to see the worst evil that is in women (fortunate in the respect that it has enabled me to read history more clearly), yet I still had to believe in the goodness of women. The best women are the hardest to know; they are identified mostly by the happiness of their husbands and the nobleness of their children. A stranger can only anticipate them, he can't find them by seeking them out. Sometimes these women seem helpless outside of their own homes. Yet without the help of one of them to whom this book is dedicated [*Rose La Touche*], I would have stopped writing and thinking years ago.

On the other hand, our era makes whatever is forward, coarse or senseless in a woman's nature seem clear to men. When I first wrote, I only knew women's emptiest enthusiasm. But later in life I had the opportunities of seeing women degraded and vindictive, which brought me face to face with the darkest gloom of ancient tragedies. I've seen women betray their homes because of lust, and break their vow of marital devotion. I've seen mothers like Medea [*who killed her children to avenge an unfaithful husband*] and daughters like Salome [*who obeyed her mother by requesting the head of John the Baptist*]. But I still believe their natures are precious, even though they can be so fatal when they go wrong. Therefore, I am not changing a word of 'Lilies.' I believe that no man has ever lived who was not rightly chastened by a woman's love, strengthened by her courage, and guided by her good sense.

I don't like to think what I might have been with the right kind of help. But since I'm taking on the role of teacher, you have a right to know what I am.

I'm not an unjust or unkind person, nor a deceitful one. I love order, honest work and peace. I think that's enough to give me the right to speak about ethics. Anything more would be better written into an autobiography, but I'm not successful or faultless enough to justify one. If you want to know more about me, you can tell something by the people in history I most identify with. I'll name three of them.

In everything that's strongest and deepest in me, what makes me fit for my work and gives light and shadow to my very being, I identify with Guido Guinicelli.

In my natural temperament and the way I think of things and people, I identify with Marmontel.

In my learned temperament and the way I think of things and people, I identify with Dean Swift.

If you can understand the natures of those three men, you can understand me. Having said this much, I am satisfied to let my life and work be remembered or forgotten, depending on their usefulness.

Denmark Hill, January 1871.

4 THE MYSTERY OF LIFE AND ITS ARTS

This is the text of a lecture that was given at the Royal College of Science in Dublin, Ireland, 1868.

When I said I would speak to you today, I was unaware of the Society's restriction on subjects I'd be allowed to talk about. The restrictions are wise and right, but they make me unable to discuss art in a way that will be useful to you. So I'm going to ignore the restriction--at least, I'll ignore the letter of the law, so to speak, but not the spirit of it. Whatever I say regarding the religion that has been the foundation of art will not single any one out. If it offends anyone, it will offend everyone, because I'm not going to mention any denominations or controversies. I don't necessarily think anyone will be offended by my proving that the best of man's crafts and arts is connected with his simple faith and sincere patriotism.

There's another reason I'm at a disadvantage and hesitate to speak frankly, not just here but everywhere. I never know how much my audience thinks I know about my subject. Maybe they're only listening to me because I've written an interesting or clever essay about it. I've had the experience (or misfortune) of putting some words ingeniously together, and even admiring my wit, and then been punished for my pride by finding out that people only enjoyed my words, but didn't care about what I was actualy saying. Fortunately, I'm getting out of the habit of using such entertaining language. Whatever I have to say, I find that I'm forced to say it in plain language. It isn't just the way I use words that has changed. My thoughts have changed, too. When I was younger, any influence I had was because I was so enthusiastic about the beauty of the clouds and their colors in the sky. I hope any influence I have now is because I'm sincerely trying to clarify and outline a different kind of cloud, the cloud spoken of in the quote, 'What is your life? It's like a vaporous cloud that's here for a little while, and then is gone.'

Very few people reach old or middle age without having a moment of change or disappointment that makes them feel how true those bitter words are. Perhaps they were startled when the sunshine faded and revealed with sudden agony that the cloud of their life was as fragile as a dream, and no more lasting than the dew. But even in our sadness, we don't always realize that life is like a cloud, not only because it's so transient, but also because it's so mysterious. Its ways are hidden in darkness, its forms and paths are just as obscure. We can't comprehend its spectacle, and we can't grasp its shadow. It is true of our cloudy life that 'man walks in a vain shadow, and worries himself for nothing.'

No matter how enthusiastic our passions have been, or how high our pride, we can't understand the most solemn characteristic of life which is like a cloud: not just transient, not just mysterious, but also powerful. In the cloud of the human soul there is a fire stronger than lightning, and a grace more precious than rain. One day the earth won't remember our good or our evil. There's an infinite separation between people whose brief life was a bright blessing like the mist of Eden, and people whose lives were no more than a changing and passing dark shadow, those who were like 'wells without water, or like clouds blown around in a storm on their way to eternal darkness.'

Some of us, though, have lived long enough to see how fast things change. The changes seem to be accelerating, bringing things closer to catastrophe. We can see it reflected in our laws, in art, and in what people believe. Now, more than ever before, we need to seriously and solemnly consider the real nature of our life, its potential and its responsibilities. Although this feeling is heavier in my own mind due to unplanned disappointments in many of my dearest goals, that in itself doesn't invalidate the feeling, although I do try to guard myself letting such feelings get out of hand. Actually, I think that, during times of new endeavors and intense change, disappointment can be a good thing. In the same way that the artist Titian saw colors deeper in twilight, we can sometimes see deeper truths in life's darker times than in its sunshine. Most of the truths I want to tell you about the works of men are sad (but still helpful) truths, and I suspect your kind Irish hearts will respond more kindly to sincere personal experience than abstract principles.

Therefore, I'll be candid about my own causes for regret, and you can make up your own minds whether I'm speaking from bitterness, or from the insight of a person who has surrendered his fondest hopes, and been frustrated in his favorite ambitions.

Between the ages of twenty to thirty, the strongest years of my life, I tried to show the excellence of J. M. W. Turner. I believed he was the greater English painter since Reynolds, and so he was. At the time, I had great faith in the truth of beauty to prevail and take its right place in usefulness and honor. I tried to bring Turner's work into this right place while he was still alive. But he knew better than I did that it was useless to tell people what they couldn't see for themselves. Even when he thanked me, he discouraged my cynically--and he died before all my efforts were even a little apparent. Yet I continued on, thinking that promoting his work would be useful to the public, even if it was too late to be of any use to him. People talked a bit about my books, and the prices (value) of modern art started to increase, so I began to enjoy a sense of gradual victory. But then (fortunately, or unfortunately?) an incident undeceived me at once. I was commissioned to show some of Turner's paintings in the National Gallery, and 300 of his nature drawings in Kensignton. They are still there, but no one ever sees them because nobody ever visits the room they hang in!

That showed me that the main effort of those ten years of my life had been wasted. I wasn't so much concerned about the years; I had at least learned my own profession (art critic) thoroughly. And I figured that the lesson I learned would enable me to use my knowledge more efficiently. But what did bother me was the unpleasant discovery that Providence would allow the most splendid artistic genius to work and die pointlessly. Something exquisite might be there in his work, but it was mixed with something else that made his work (and genius) invisible to most ordinary eyes. His paintings might have a strange excellence, but it was mingled with faults that rendered its virtues fruitless. Thus, the glory of his work was not only invisible, but perishable. The gift and grace of it were as unappreciated as snow would be in the hot summer, or as rain that might spoil the harvest.

That was the first mystery of life to me. But even while my best energy was being used to study painting, I was also studying architecture on the side. This study might not have been as enthusiastic, but it was more prudent, and gained me more support. One of the reasons I wanted my last art lecture to be in Ireland is because I could speak while standing near the beautiful (Trinity College) engineer's school at your college (Royal College of Science in Dublin). That building was the first time I had the joy of seeing of the principles I had been trying to teach! Unfortunately, it is now nothing more to me than a beautifully draped monument to architect Benjamin Woodward, one of the most sincere souls who ever devoted his life to art, and one of my truest and dearest friends. [*Woodward had died in 1861, seven years before this lecture.*] But it wasn't just here in Ireland that I received help and support from Irish geniuses. Thomas Deane was entrusted along with Woodward to build the Oxford University Museum of Natural History. The finest details of the work were done by sculptors who were born and trained in Ireland. The first window of the front of the building for studying the natural science of England, which goes along well with literature, was carved by an Irish sculptor from my design.

You might think that a man shouldn't talk about disappointment in a field he's had so much success in. If Woodward was here, I wouldn't have spoken like that. But his gentle, passionate spirit was thwarted from fulfilling its purposes, and all the work we did together was for nothing. Maybe something will come of it in the future. But the architecture we tried so hard to introduce is inconsistent with today's irresponsible luxury, industrialism that deforms, and the squalid misery of modern cities. During the beginning of its formative period, with the help of religious sentiment, especially in England, that sort of architecture got some attention. Even today, behind an ugly engine furnace, or utilitarian railroad bank, you can sometimes glimpse its graceful delicacy in disharmony with the modern world, and if you look hard enough, you can see its floral carvings under layers of soot. I felt responsible for the beautiful schools I loved, but it hadn't done them any lasting good. So this part of my life was also wasted. I turned my attention away from the iron streets and crystal palaces constructed by men, and returned to the natural carvings of majestic mountains, and color of flowers.

There are other failures over the years I could tell you about, but I won't try your patience by showing you more reasons for my discouragement. I'd rather tell you its results. Many men, after this kind of disappointment, would declare that life itself is useless--nothing but vanity. Since it has disappointed them, they think it will disappoint everyone, or that any pleasure it holds is all in the imagination, but the essence of it--the cloud--has no strength or fire inside it. It's only a painting of a cloud to be enjoyed, but not relied on. Alexander Pope expressed this feeling beautifully:

> Meanwhile, opinion paints with various colors
> These painted clouds that make our days more beautiful.
> Hope fills in each lack of happiness.
> Pride fills in each sense of emptiness.
> Hope continues building as fast as knowledge is destroying.
> Bubbly joy still laughs in the cup of foolishness.
> When one pleasure is over, there's another to look forward to.
> Not one vanity is given in vain.

But failure has had the opposite effect on me. The more life disappointed me, the more solemn and amazing it seemed to me. Contrary to Alexander Pope's poem, the vanity of life *was* given in vain--but there was something real behind the veil, and that was not vanity. That cloud was not a painted one; it was terrible and impervious. It was not a mirage that would vanish as soon as I got nearer to it, but a pillar of darkness, and I wasn't allowed to get near it. I saw that my failure as well as my successes that seemed so trivial that they were worse than failure both came because I did not earnestly try to understand the whole law and meaning of existence, and did not try to bring it to a noble and right end. At the same time, I also saw that all enduring success in art (or anything else) came from the power of lower purposes, not because the art was worthless, but because of a solemn faith that human nature could make progress, or because of the hope, no matter how dimly grasped, that the finite (worthless) part would be swallowed up in immortality some day. In fact, the arts themselves had never become vitally strong or honorable except for when they proclaimed this hope of immortality, and when they served a great and fair religion, or unselfish patriotism, or law of life that is the foundation of religion.

The truest and most necessary thing I've ever said (and the most misunderstood and misapplied) is that art can never be right unless its motive is right. This is how people misunderstand: weak painters who have never really learned their craft and can't even draw a straight line will come up to me and complain, 'Look at my picture. It must be good since I had such a wonderful motive. I put my whole heart into it, and it took years to figure out how to work it out.' The only proper response to such people, if anyone was heartless enough to say it, is, 'You? You couldn't figure out a thing even if you had a hundred years! You haven't got the mind for it. Even if you had the best of motives, you can't paint even an inch of the work because you don't have the skill to do it.'

It's more important to address those who *do* have the skill, or are capable of learning it: 'You have this gift, and it's a powerful gift. Serve your nation faithfully with it. It is a greater responsibility than ships or armies. A captain who abandoned his ship would be less guilty of treason to his people than you will be if you cast away your glorious ability by serving the devil with it instead of helping your fellow men. Ships and armies can be replaced, but a great mind is a curse to the earth forever once it's misused.'

That's what I meant by saying that art must have noble motives. I also said art had never prospered (and could never prosper) unless it had this kind of true purpose, and devoted itself to proclaiming divine law and truth. Yet I saw that art always seemed to fail to do this. Poetry, sculpture and painting are great when they teach us about divine truths, but they never seem to teach us anything accurate about the gods. Instead, they always seem to betray their trust just when they reach the moment of truth. Just when their powers reach their climax, they become agents of pride and lust. Meanwhile, I saw with some surprise that we, as viewers and hearers, are unable to conquer the apathy within ourselves any better than the artists who are supposed to teach us. Every work of art can only teach wisdom and correctness when it is consistent with a proper understanding of the purpose of life, but all of us seem to be floating in a sluggish dream. Our hearts are fat, our eyes are heavy, and our ears are closed, which prevents the inspiration of art from reaching us. So how can we see with our eyes and understand with our ears and be healed?

This extreme apathy in all of us is the first great mystery of life. It gets in the way of everything we see, and every virtue. It is perplexing. It's understandable that our pursuits and amusements should have no motive. But that life itself should have no motive? How is it that we don't care to find out what life leads to, or prevent life from being taken away from us forever? This is a great mystery! Imagine that I called one of you by name and told you that a certain estate with a beautiful mansion and surrounding land had been left to you with some odd strings attached, but I didn't know how extensive the property was, or even where it was. Maybe it was in India, or in California, or England, or maybe even in Australia. All I knew for sure is that it was a large estate, and if you didn't find out the terms under which it was left to you soon, you would lose it altogether. Do you think you would sit back, content to have only that vague knowledge, if you were able to find out more? Wouldn't you would go to extreme lengths to get more information, and never rest until you knew where the place was, and what it was like? Now, what if you were young and you found out that you could only have this estate if you perservered in an orderly and industious life for a number of years? And what if the amount of the estate you inherited, whether you got $160,000 a year or $485,000, or nothing at all, depended on your right conduct? Wouldn't it be strange if you never bothered to try to satisfy the conditions in any way, or even to find out what the conditions were, but continued to live as you always had without ever wondering if your chances of acquiring the estate were increasing or decreasing? Of course, this is actually true for most educated people in Christian countries. Nearly every person in this room professes to believe even more than this. You know that an unlimited estate is in your eternal future if you please God, Who owns it. You also know that perpetual misery (Hell) awaits those who displease this Divine Land-Holder of heaven. Yet not even one in a thousand cares to spend even ten mintes a day thinking about this estate, considering how beautiful it might be, or what they'll do there, or what kind of life they should live now if they ever want to get there.

I imagine you think you care. In fact, you're probably offended that I'm talking about it. You came to hear me talk about the Art of this world, not the Life of the next world. Maybe you're annoyed at me for talking about something you hear in church every Sunday. But don't worry; before you go, I'll tell you something about paintings, sculpture, pottery, and everything else you prefer to hear about than the Other World. Or perhaps you're thinking, 'We want you to talk about paintings and pottery because we know that you know something about them. You don't know anything about the Other World.' That's true; I don't. But neither do you. Can you answer a single question confidently about that Other World? Are you even sure there *is* a heaven? Are you sure there's a Hell? Do you have any certainty that real men are vanishing from before your very faces and descending from these very streets into eternal fire? Do you have any certainty that they aren't? Do you have any certainty that when you die yourself, you're going to be delivered from all sorrow, enriched with all virtue, graced with all happiness, and raised into eternal friendship with a King who is so great that He makes kings of this earth seem like grasshoppers, and makes the nations they rule seem as inconsequential as the dust on the ground? Are you sure of all these things? If you're not sure, are you concerned enough about it to find out? If not, how can anything we do be right? How can anything we do be wise? What honor can there possibly be in those Arts that amuse us so much? What profit can there be in the stuff we own and enjoy?

Is this not a great Mystery of Life?

Going even farther, maybe you think it's a good thing in general that people don't earnestly or anxiously dwell on those kinds of questions about the future because, if this kind of thought occupied people's minds, the business of the day couldn't be done. That might be true. But you'd think that, at the very least, the greatest and wisest people who are evidently supposed to teach everyone else, would set themselves apart to seek out whatever could be known for sure about the future destinies of humans. Then they could teach this to the rest of us, not in a pretentious or cryptic way, but with the clearest and most solemnly sincere words.

During the Christian era, the highest representatives of great men who have done this, who have tried to search out these deep truths and tell the rest of us, have been Dante and Milton. No one else is in the same class as they are when it comes to earnest thought and mastery of language. I'm not counting those who are set apart as priests and preachers whose job it is to teach us creeds and doctrines. I'm only talking about men who try to discover and present the facts about the Other World, as far as human intellect is able. Clergymen might be able to tell us how to get there, but only those two poets have had any success in trying to find out or related in definite words what we'll see when we get there, what we'll be like, and what else lives in those upper and under Worlds.

And what have they told us? The way Milton tells the most important event that happens in his account--the fall of the angels--makes it clear that it's hard for him to believe himself. It is based on Hesiod's story of the war of the younger gods against the Titans. The rest of his poem (Paradise Lost) is a pleasant story, and he obviously uses every literary device to tell it; not a single fact of his story is consistent with any living faith. Dante's impression is much more intense, and he can't escape from it even for an instant. It's only a vision, but it's the wildest vision a human mind ever had--a dream in which every ugly fantasy of pagan tradition is included and added to, and the future of the Christian church, represented by religion's most sacred symbols, becomes submissive to the praise of one Florentine girl (Beatrice), or understood with her help.

As I struggle with my own apathy and lethargy, and awaken to the meaning and power of life, it seems more amazing to me every day that men like Milton and Dante would dare play with such precious truths (or maybe the most deadly lies?). With such a huge audience reading them with pleased ears and passionate hearts, they could be informing or deceiving the whole world. So many souls are submitting to their teachings, hungry for true bread of life, but all they do is play on sweetly tuned flutes. They label the councils of hell with fancy names. They write pretty songs to describe the paths of various suns. Prophets hid their faces from the entrance to eternity, and the angels themselves would love to look in, but Milton and Dante write about it with trivial characters made up out of their academic imaginations, and with sad glimpses of desperate faith in a doomed mortal love affair.

Is this not a great Mystery of Life?

There's even more. Both of these men had distorted frames of mind and were thwarted in their search for truth. They had intellectual struggles. Because of controversy, or personal grief, they were unable to discern where their own ambition reshaped what they said about the moral law. Or else their own agony and anger was mingled with episodes they wrote about from personal experience. But there have been greater men than these who were too great to be challenged--men like Homer and Shakespeare whose personality is so unrecognizable in their works that their own nature disappears and becomes a mystery to future generations, like the traditions of lost heathen gods. When they write, they seem unoffended and uncondemning, so that they present all of human nature as a pathetic weakness that they don't struggle with, or a depressing and passing strength that they don't dare praise. They write about both pagan and Christian societies this way. It doesn't matter whether you've read a lot or a little of Homer or Shakespeare--you have been influenced by them because everything around us, both tangibly [*such as our very language?*] and the way we think has been shaped by them. Greek gentlemen were educated with Homer's literature. Roman gentlemen were educated by Greeks [*who were educated with Homer's literature*]. Italian, French and English gentlemen have been educated by Roman literature and Roman principles. And what about Shakespeare? Since his time, every person's creative intellect has been measured by how much he has learned from Shakespeare. These two men--Homer and Shakespeare--are centers of moral intelligence. What convictions do they relay to us about what's most important to understand? What is their hope and culmination of joy? What advice do they give us, or warnings? What is dearest to their hearts, and inspires their lasting words? Can they offer any peace for our unrest? Can they offer any redemption for our misery?

Let's take Homer first. Is there any sadder image of human fate than his Iliad? The main features in Achilles' character are an intense desire for justice and a tender affection. Achilles is continually helped by the wisest of the gods, and his heart burns with a desire for justice, yet, through undisciplined passion, he becomes the most unjust of men. Though he has the deepest tenderness in his heart, through undisciplined passion, he becomes the cruelest of men. He is intense in love and friendship, but he loses his mistress, and then his friend. For the sake of one, he surrenders his own armies to death. For the sake of the other, he surrenders everything else. Will a man lay down his life for his friend? Yes, Achilles, born and taught of a goddess, gives up his kingdom, his country, and his life for a friend who is already dead! He casts the innocent and the guilty along with himself into a pit of slaughter, and is finally killed by his most contemptible enemy.

Is this not a great Mystery of Life?

What, then, does Shakespeare, our own English poet, have to tell us after fifteen hundred years of Christianity's influence over the world? Are his words any more cheerful than the heathen Homer's? Is his hope any closer? Is his trust more certain? Does fate seem any happier? No! His main difference from Homer is this: he doesn't recognize *any* gods at hand to deliver man. It is by trivial chance, a moment of foolishness, a misunderstood message, a fool's unreasonableness, or a traitor's trap, that his strongest and most righteous characters are ruined, and die without any word of hope. I admit that he attributes the strength and sincerity of habitual devotion to his gentle and just characters. Katharine sees a bright vision of angels while she's on her death-bed [*Henry VIII Act IV*]. Henry V, the great soldier-king, as he stands by the few men who died in battle, says, 'We are in God's hand, brother, not in theirs.' But notice that Shakespeare's characters who meditate with the deepest spirit, and who mourn with the deepest passion, don't say any words like these, or have any consolations like these in their hearts. In pagan tradition [*Homer*] the helpful presence of the gods is the source of heroic strength in battle, in exile and in death. But our great Christian poet only writes about an awareness of a moral law through which 'the gods are just' when they punish us by making whips out of our own temptations. And when we feebly and blindly begin on a wrong path, destiny concludes the path into a sure doom. When we make a mistake, fate forces us to admit that 'there's a divinity that shapes our ends,' no matter how crudely we try to sculpt them ourselves.

Is this not a great Mystery of Life?

Alrighty then. Whatever this human life is supposed to be, or is going to be, wise religious men tell us nothing trustworthy, and wise thinking men tell us nothing that can give us peace. But there's a third group of men we can consider: wise practical men. Poets who sing about heaven have told us their dreams. Poets who sing about life on earth sing sad, despairing songs. But there's one more group of men. These men don't see visions, and aren't sensitive to sorrow, but they do have a firm purpose. They are skilled in business, educated in everything that can be known from hands-on learning. Their hearts and hopes are fully in this present world. Therefore, we can surely learn from them how to comfortably live in the world. What do they have to teach us? These politicians, capitalists, and businessmen weigh the earth and its resources and determine whether it will turn a profit. Surely they know the world, and what seems mysterious to us is no secret to them. Surely they can show us how to live while we're here, and how to get what's best from the present world.

The best way for me to tell you their answer is to share a dream I once had. I may not be a poet, but I do have dreams sometimes. I dreamed I was at a child's springtime party. All kinds of entertainment had been provided by the wise, kind host. The party was at an impressive house with beautiful gardens around it. The children were free to roam the house and gardens and do whatever they felt like doing all afternoon. They didn't know much about what the next day might bring. I thought some of them seemed a little scared because there was a chance they were going to be sent to a new school that gave exams, but they kept that out of their minds as much as they could and tried hard to enjoy themselves. The garden had all kinds of lovely flowers, green grassy banks to rest on, smooth lawns to play on, pleasant streams and woods, and rocky places for climbing. The children were happy for a little while, but then they started to separate into little groups, and then each group declared that it wanted part of garden exclusively to itself, and no one else should be allowed to use their part of the garden. Then they argued heatedly about who would get each part, and, finally, the boys did the 'practical' thing and started fighting in the flower-beds until there was hardly a flower left standing. Then, out of spite, they trampled each other's parts of the garden. The girls cried brokenheartedly, and they all finally collapsed, out of breath, in the ruin, and waited until it was time for them to be taken home.

Meanwhile, the children inside the house had been enjoying themselves. There was music to dance to, a library with all kinds of amusing books, a museum full of interesting seashells, animals, and birds, a workshop with tools for building, elaborate and fancy dresses for the girls to dress up in, microscopes, kaleidoscopes, every kind of toy imaginable, and the dining room table was loaded with all kinds of treats.

But in the midst of all of this, it suddenly struck the more 'practical' children that they wanted some of the brass-headed nails the chairs were studded with. So they set to work to pull them out. Soon, all the other children who had been reading or looking at shells, decided to do the same thing. Soon nearly all the children were spraining their fingers to try and pry the brass nails out of the chairs. When they had gotten all of them out, they still weren't satisfied. Everybody wanted someone else's nails. Finally, the really 'practical' and sensible children announced that nothing else mattered except getting plenty of brass nails. They said that the books, cakes, and microscopes were of no use unless they could be exchanged for brass nails. And finally they started to fight over the brass nails just like the others had fought over the garden. Here and there, a rejected child slunk away into a corner and tried to find a little peace and quiet with a book. But all the practical children thought of nothing but counting nails all afternoon--even though they knew they wouldn't be allowed to carry even a single nail away with them! Yet all they could say was, 'Who has the most nails? I have a hundred, and you only have fifty,' or 'I have a thousand, but you have two thousand. I'm not leaving until I have as many as you.' Finally they made so much noise that I woke up. I thought to myself, 'what a false dream, children aren't like that!' The child is the father of the man [*because men grow from and evolve out of children*]. They are wiser. Children don't do such foolish things; only grown men do.

There's still one more group of people to be considered. We've asked wise religious men but they couldn't help us. The wise thoughtful men and the wise wordly 'practical' men couldn't help us. But there's still another group. In the middle of this charade of empty religion, and pathetic reflection, and furious and disastrous ambition and bickering over dust, there's still one more group of people. Everyone else depends on this group. These are those who have determined (or providence has determined for them) that they will do something useful. Whatever happens to them here, or whatever might be provided for them in the hereafter, they will at least work to deserve the food God gives them by earning it honorably. No matter how far they have fallen from the purity or peace of Eden, they will continue to do their duty in this earthly world, even though they no longer enjoy it. They continue to prune and maintain the wilderness even if they can no longer prune and maintain the garden [*of Eden*].

These are the people who cut wood and carry water, are bent under burdens or wounded from whips, they dig, weave, plant, build, engrave wood, chisel stone, and mold iron. They are responsible for all food, clothing, homes, furniture, and entertainment--not only for themselves but for all of us. These are people whose deeds may be good even though they may not say much. Their lives are useful, even if they might be short. They are worthy of honor even though they're humble. Surely these people can give us some clear message that will pierce the mystery of life.

Yes, they do teach us a lesson. But, sadly, I have to admit--or, actually, I'm thrilled to say that you can only receive their message by joining them, not by just thinking about them.

You wanted me to talk about art. But the main thing I have to say is that art can't just be talked about. The fact that there's so much talk about it suggests that it's being done badly, or that it simply can't be done well. No real painter ever talks much about his art. The greatest artists say nothing. [*Those who can, do, and those who can't--talk about it?*] Even Sir Joshua Reynolds is no exception. He wrote about what he couldn't do himself, but was silent about what he actually did well.

The moment a person can actually *do* his work, he stops talking about it. Words become empty for him, mere theories.

Does a bird theorize about nest building, or boast about it after it's built? All good work is done that way: eagerly, easily, modestly. Those who do the best things have an inner, involuntary ability that's similar to an animal's instinct. In fact, I'm certain that in the most perfect human artists, reason doesn't override instinct, but accompanies an instinct that is as divinely superior to animal instinct as the human body is superior to an animal body. A great singer doesn't sing with less instinct than a nightingale, but with more--but the singer's instinct is more varying, more applicable, and more within the control of the artist. A great architect doesn't build with less instinct than a beaver or a bee, but with more--but the architect's instinct has an inborn intuition about proportion that encompasses all kinds of beauty, and a divine cleverness in his skill that can improvise when he builds. Whether the human's instinct is more or less, or similar or different, the gist of it is that human art depends first on instinct, and then on practice and scientfic method, and then on imagination that has been disciplined with reflection. The man who possesses this kind of genius knows he can't explain it in words, and the true critic knows that it's undefinable and can only be understood through long years of hard work. The making of the world--hills upon hills, mountains upon mountains--can you make a copy of it by talking about it? Can you even carry us up a mountain by talking? No, but you can guide us up. It has to be done step by step, if it's done at all, and even then, it's best done in silence. Those of you who have toured the Alps know how a bad guide chatters on and on, saying, 'put your foot there,' or 'be careful how you balance yourself on that ledge.' A good guide walks on quietly, without a word, but he watches to see if you need help, and he offers a strong arm when necessary.

Art is taught in the same slow way, as long as you trust your guide and let his strong arm help you when necessary. But is there any art teacher you can trust that much? You certainly don't trust me. As I already said, I'm fully aware that you asked me to speak because I can talk, not because I know art. If I told you anything unusual, you wouldn't believe it, and yet I would only be useful to you if I told you unusual things. I could be of infinite use to you by saying something brief, if you'd believe it. But you wouldn't believe it, because you wouldn't like [*nor accept*] the most useful thing I could say. For example, you're crazy about Gustave Dore. What if I told you emphatically that Dore's art was bad--not because it's weak, or because it fails, but because of dreadful power [*ability?*] His art has the powers of the Furies and harpies mingled, enraging and polluting so much that the longer you look at it, the less possible it will be for you to perceive pure or beautiful art. What would be the use of telling you that? Would you look at Dore's pictures any less? No, you'd look at them even more. On the other hand, if I wanted to, I could put you in a good mood if I wanted to. I know what you like, and I know how to praise it to make you like it even more. I could talk to you about moonlight, and twilight, and spring flowers, and autumn leaves, and how motherly Raphael's Madonnas are, and how majestic Michelangelo's sibyls are, how pious Angelico's saints are, and how delicious Correggio's cherubs are. Even as old as I am, I could play you a tune that I know you would dance to. But neither you nor I would be any better or wiser. Even if we gained some knowledge, that knowledge would be of no practical use. When it comes to teaching, the arts are different from science because their strength isn't merely on facts you can list, but on an attitude that needs to be instilled. You don't get art by thinking hard, and you can't explain it by choosing words accurately. Art is the instinctive and necessary result of talent, and that talent can only be developed through the minds of one generation after another until it finally bursts forth under the proper social conditions that are slowly evolving. Entire ages of history are summed up, and the passions of thousands of dead populations are concentrated in a single noble art. If that noble art were here, we would recognize it and rejoice. We wouldn't need to hear lectures about it. Since it isn't here among us, we'll have to go back to the root of it--where the stem is still alive, although some branches of it have died off.

And now, I hope you'll forgive me for pointing out that if we went back to the stem of a vital art that has decayed, we'd find a more notable obstruction in the arts of Ireland than in any other European country. In the 700's, Ireland had an art school specializing in manuscripts and sculpture which was without equal. It could have advanced to the highest triumphs in architecture and painting. But its nature had a fatal flaw that halted it, and halted it conspicuously. In a lecture I gave tracing the progress of European schools from their infancy to their maturity, there are two characteristic examples of early art that were equally skillful. In one case, the skill was progressing. In the other case, there was a pause. In the progressive skill, the work was receptive to correction, and even hungry for it. The other work inherently rejected correction. To illustrate, I showed a picture of Eve that was open to improvement, and a picture of an uncorrectable angel. I am sorry to say, the angel was an Irish picture.

And here is the fatal difference. Both pieces equally fell short of the needs of fact [*accurate line and proportion?*]. But the Lombardic [*Lombards: German tribe who settled in Italy*] Eve knew she was all wrong, and the Irish angel thought he was alright. The eager Lombardic sculptor, even when he was firmly fixed on his childish idea, showed by the broken irregular touches of the features and the visible struggle to create softer lines in the form, that he knew what beauty was, but could not render it the way he wanted to. You could see his frustrated effort in the conscious imperfection of every line. But the Irish psalter painter had drawn his angel in happy smugness. He put red dots on the palm of each hand, rounded the eyes into perfect circles, and, I'm sorry to say, left out the mouth altogether--all with complete self-satisfaction.

Would you be offended if I wonder whether this halt in ancient Irish art might point to a national flaw of character that has also halted your power as a nation in some way? I've seen a lot of Irish character. In fact, I've observed it closely, because I love it. And I think that the most likely flaw is that you, being generous-hearted and having the best of intentions, don't actually look into external principles of right and wrong. You assume that because you mean to do the right thing, you must automatically be doing it. So you unwittingly end up doing wrong in ignorance. Then when you experience the consequences of doing the wrong thing, you don't make the connection and you fly off into a rage and complain about injustice. You feel entirely innocent, so you go even farther astray, until you're doing all kinds of bad things with a clear conscience.

Rest assured, I have no intention of saying that, in relations between Ireland and England, you've always been wrong and England has always been right. In fact, I think that in issues of principles and enforcing law, you've usually been right and England has been wrong. England has sometimes been wrong in misunderstanding you, and sometimes been outright sinful towards you. Generally, when there's a dispute between countries, the stronger country is more in the wrong and the weaker country is only wrong to a lesser degree. But England is usually ready to admit its own guilt, and Ireland never does!

Getting back to the broader question, what do the arts and duties of life teach us about life's mystery? This is their first lesson: the more beautiful the art, the more it's basically done by people who think they aren't doing it right--they're trying to interpret a law they can't quite grasp, and pin down a loveliness they can't quite reach. The more they strive for it, the farther away it seems. At the same time, in a deeper sense, this art is also done by people who know they're on the right track. The very fact that they feel they can't reach what they aim for shows that they know they're aiming for the right thing, and their continued sense of failure shows that their eyes are more clearly seeing the most sacred laws of truth. [*He who aims for the unreachable stars gets higher than he who aims for the trees?*]

The second lesson is plain, but very precious: whenever life's art and work is done in a spirit of striving against lawlessness and whenever we do whatever we need to do honorably and well, it brings us happiness (at least, as much happiness as man's nature is capable of). When man attempts to pursue happiness by any other path, the result is disappointment or destruction. That's because there is no rest or satisfaction for ambition and passion. Even the most wonderful pleasures of youth are forgotten in a darkness that's more intense than their past brightness, and the most pure and glorious love too often only inflames life with pain. But stepping from the lowest level to each succeeding higher level through honest work brings peace. Ask any worker in the field, or skilled craftsman, or anyone who works intensely with bronze or stone or color. Any of these who are true workmen will tell you that the law of heaven is very fair. They will say that their obedience was rewarded as long as it was done faithfully according to the command, 'Whatever your hand finds to do, do it with all your strength.'

These are the two great and consistent lessons that workers teach us about the mystery of life. But there's another lesson, a sadder lesson, that they can't teach us. We have to read that lesson on their tombstones.

'Do it with all your strength.' There have been millions and millions of people who have obeyed that law, who have put every breath and fiber of their being into their work, devoted every hour, exhausted every skill, and have handed down their uncompleted thoughts when they died. Although they are dead, their memory and example still speak to us. After six thousand years of labor and sorrow, what has all this 'strength' of humanity accomplished? What has it done? Let's look at three main occupations and arts, one at a time, and consider what they've accomplished. Let's start with the most majestic one: agriculture, the art of kings. Six thousand years have passed since man was appointed to till the ground from which we were made. And in that time, how much has been cultivated? Of that which is cultivated, how much is cultivated well or wisely? In the very center of Europe, in the forests and valleys of Switzerland, the untamed Alpine rivers still run wild in devastation. The marshes that a few hundred men could make useful in a year, still cause their helpless inhabitants to be thrown into a panic [*from flood? landslides?*] And this is in the middle of Europe! Meanwhile, on the western coast of Africa, which was once called the Garden of the

Hesperides, an Arab woman not too long ago ate her own child because she was starving from a famine! We in England have wealth that the orient only dreamed of, but we couldn't even come up with some rice for those starving people. Instead, we stood by while 500,000 people died of hunger.

Next, let's look at weaving, which is the art of queens. It was honored by noble heathen women in the form of Athena, and honored by Hebrews in the Proverbs: 'She makes thread with her hands and weaves her own cloth. . . She makes coverings for herself; her clothes are made of linen and other expensive material.' In six thousand years, what have we accomplished with weaving? In that time, we could have covered every wall in the world with purple tapestry, and given warm clothes to every cold, unclothed person. What have we done? One would think our fingers were too weak to twist a few threads together to even make a shred of clothing for ourselves. We fill our rivers with waterwheels to generate power, and choke the air with smoke to fuel spinning wheels in our factories. Has this clothed all the needy? The streets of Europe's cities are filled with thread-bare clothes and dirty rags, beautiful children are left wretched and dressed in tatters. Even Nature clothes birds and wolves more honorably. The snow of winter puts a robe of white over everything you have not covered. Those you have not cloaked warmly are shrouded in death from the cold. Every gust of bitter winter wind carries up to heaven the cries of those poor souls, who will witness against you, saying, 'I was naked and you didn't clothe me.'

Last of all, let's look at the art of building: Architecture. This is the strongest, proudest, most orderly and enduring of all man's arts. This art continues to accumulate because it doesn't perish or have to be replaced. If it's built well, it will stand longer than the precariously-balanced rocks, and will prevail longer than the crumbling hills. A community's pride and most hallowed principles are tied to its buildings. Cultures have recorded their history and strength into their architecture, satisfied their enthusiasm, fortified their defenses, defined and personalized homes for themselves. In six thousand years, what have we accomplished with architecture? Of our best buildings, all that's left is ruins that litter our fields and fallen stones that clog our streams. What do we have to show for it? We are such constructive and progressive beings, with commanding brains and skillful hands. We're capable of fellowship, we desire fame, yet [*in 1860's pre-air-conditioning days*] we haven't even learned how to make our homes as comfortable as termites, who build climate-controlled mounds. And we haven't achieved what coral-building sea worms have. They're ignorant, yet the surf rages against the coral reefs they leave behind, and the sea can't conquer those reefs. But all that's left of the noblest cultures of man is ridges of formless ruins. Ants and moths have an individual cell for each of their babies, but we have little ones lying in festering heaps of slums--homes that consume them like graves. Every night, the voices of the homeless rise up to heaven, saying, 'I was a stranger, and you did not take me in.'

Will it always be like this? Will our life always be without profit and without possession? Will the strength of all mankind be as barren as death? Will man's hard work always be cast away like wild figs that drop from the tree too soon? Is the desire of the eyes and the pride of life merely an illusion? And if it is, might it be possible to have a nobler dream to live for? Poets, prophets, wise men and scribes might not have told us what the next world is like, but they have told us a lot about the life we're living here on earth. They've had their dreams and desires, too, and we've laughed at them and mocked them. They've dreamed of mercy and justice, they've dreamed of peace and goodwill. They've dreamed of work that isn't wasted, and undisturbed rest. They've dreamed of having enough food for everyone, and some to spare. They've dreamed of wise advice, and prudent laws. They've dreamed of happy parents, strong children, and respected old people. And we have scorned their visions, and called them useless, ineffective, unrealistic and not doable. So what have we accomplished with our practical realities? Hungry, unclothed and homeless mobs are the result of all our worldly wisdom--is that better than the visions of our dreamers? Is our strength and mighty labor more effective than the ideals of our dreamers? Or have we been wandering through a rainbow of ignorant glee, chasing ghosts of the tombs instead of pursuing visions of God? Have we been pursuing the imaginations of our evil hearts instead of God's advice, so that our lives, more like the smoke of hell than the clouds of heaven, are like 'a vapor that appears for a little while, and then vanishes'?

But do our lives vanish? Do you know? Will our troubled labor for nothing result in a long rest of nothingness in the grave? Are you sure that the smoky cloud that coils for nothing won't turn into the smoke of torment that rises forever? Does anyone know that there is no fear, no hope, no desire, no work where they're going? Be that as it may, shouldn't you be sure of your present life even if you can't be sure what happens after death? As long as your hearts are fully in this world, why not devote your hearts fully and wisely to good purpose in the world? Make sure you have hearts--real, feeling hearts--and healthy hearts to give to the world. Just because you have no heaven to look forward to, that's no reason to be ignorant about this wonderful, infinite world we have right here that's within your grasp. Your days may be numbered, and the dark nothingness of death might be certain, but that doesn't mean you have to live like a degraded animal. You don't have to live like a worm or a moth just because you're returning to dust the same as they are. We don't have to live like them. We might only live for a few thousand days, or maybe only hundreds--maybe even less than that. No matter how long our life is, the longest life will seem like a short moment, or the twinkling of an eye, when we look back on it. Nevertheless, we are *people*, not insects. We are living spiritual beings, not passing clouds. God 'makes the wind carry His messages, and makes the short burst of fire his servant.' Can we do any less than the elements that serve God? Let's work like men while we have the life of men. As we grab hold of the little bit of time from eternity we are allowed, let's also grab a little bit of passion from Immortality, even though our lives are merely a vapor that appears for a little while and then disappears.

But some of you don't believe this. You don't think the cloud of life has an end. You think that the cloud of life will float along the floor of heaven, revealed and spotlighted, on that day when He comes with clouds and every eye sees Him. You believe that some day, in a few years, the judgment will come for every one of us, and God's books will be opened. If that's true, then there's more than that which must also be true. Is there only one day of judgment? For us, every day is a day of judgment. Every day writes its unchangeable verdict in God's book. Do you think that judgment waits until you go to your grave? No, it waits at the door to your house, and at the corners of your street. We're in the middle of judgment; every insect we crush is judging us. Every pleasure that deceives us judges us even while it indulges us! So, while we're alive, let's do the work of man since our lives are not like vapor and will not disappear.

'The work of man'--what exactly *is* that? It's easy for any of us to figure out when we're in a frame of mind to actually *do* it. But too many are thinking more about what we're going to get than what we're going to do, and even the best of us are stuck in Ananias's deadly sin of wanting to keep back something for ourselves. We continue to talk about taking up our cross as if the only consideration was the weight of it, as if the cross was only something that had to be carried rather than a thing to be crucified on. 'Those who are His have crucified their flesh, along with its affections and lusts.' Do you think that means that in times of national anxiety, religious trial, or perplexity in every area that threatens the hope of humanity, that we'll just keep on joking, taking it easy, not rolling up our sleeves to work or even lifting a finger, in order to save the world? Or does it mean being ready to leave our home, our land, our family, and even our life if it comes to that? Some of us have made our lives so joyless that we'd think nothing of throwing those lives away. But what about about our position in life? How many of us are ready to give that up? That's usually the great objection when someone considers something they could do: they don't want to give up their position in life.

Those of who really are unable to leave their position--meaning, those who can only live and pay their bills by keeping a particular career or salary job--already *have* something to do. Their primary concern should be making sure they do it honestly and to the best of their ability. But most people who are concerned about giving up a position in life are thinking of the fancy cars and servants and expensive homes they're paying for. All I can say is, if God specifically put you in that kind of position (which is doubtful), God is right now calling you out of it. In the gospels, Levi's position in life was collecting taxes, Peter's was fishing on the shore of Galilee, and Paul's was in the private rooms of the High Priest. But each of them had to leave that position, and with extremely short notice.

No matter what our position in life may be, during this time of perplexity, we who want to do our duty should first of all determine to live on as little as we can, and secondly, we should do all the restorative work we can to help, and spare everything we can to do whatever worthwhile work we can.

And worthwhile work means feeding people, and then clothing them, and then making sure they have a roof over their heads, and last of all, enriching them with art, science or any other thinking kind of amusement.

The first item on my list is feeding people. Don't be deceived by what you hear about 'indiscriminate charity' [*or enabling an entitlement class*]. God's command isn't to feed the 'deserving hungry' or 'hardworking hungry,' or even the pleasant, well-intentioned hungry. The command is simply to feed the hungry. It's a true principle that if a person won't work, he should not eat. Think about that every time you sit down to your dinner. Before you pray a blessing over your food, ask yourself, 'How much real work have I done today for this dinner?' But the right way to enforce that principle on those under you as well as on yourselves, isn't to let both honest destitute and career charity people stay hungry together. The solution is to accurately identify and separate the career charity people from the rest. Make sure that those people do some kind of work before they eat. But before you can do that, you have to be sure you have food to give. That means putting a plan in place to create huge agricultural operations and donation organizations to produce, store and distribute healthy food so that famine will never be possible among civilized people ever again. This alone provides plenty of work to be done for those who are inclined to put their efforts in that direction.

The second item is clothing people. By that I mean urging everyone you can influence to be neat and clean, and providing the means for them to do that. If people refuse, you can withdraw your effort towards them. But see to it that any children you can influence don't grow up with those habits and that those who are willing to be neat and clean have the encouragement and the means to be. It would be most effective to gradually adopt a system where people consistently dressed in the same style according to their position in society, and changes in fashions would be restricted within certain limits [*in other words, a complete overhaul of the fashion industry*]. Right now, this seems impossible, but even the impossibility is because of our own vanity, silliness, and desire to look like something we're not. And I firmly believe that such pretentious pride and shallowness is something Christians *can* conquer.

The third item is making sure people have a roof over their heads. You might think this should have been first, but I made it third because we have to feed people where and when we find them in need, and worry about lodging them after that. Providing housing means a lot of persuasive efforts to change laws, and removing special interests [*lobbies, pressure groups*] that stand in the way. Then the housing we do have [*slums*] should be cleaned up and fixed up. Then we need to build attractive, sturdy homes in small groups proportioned to the need, fenced in to keep slum sprawl from seeping in and taking over. There should be a brisk, clean street through it, and a border of beautiful garden around the fence so that anyone in any part of the little community can get to fresh air, green grass, and a view of the horizon within just a few minutes' walk. This would be the final goal. [*This plan sounds like Walt Disney's City of Tomorrow. Seriously. He was an INFP visionary whose dreams went beyond cartoons and theme parks.*] But for right now, we need to take immediate action to make every small improvement we can: mend leaking roofs, patch holes in fences, shore up leaning walls, level lopsided floors. We should establish cleanliness and order with our own hands every day. Then the fine arts will naturally follow. I myself once washed an entire flight of steps at an inn with a bucket of soapy water and a broom, and I never drew a better sketch than I did that afternoon.

These three (food, clothes, housing) are the first necessities of civilized life. The Christian command is to be directly involved in meeting one of these needs--by helping as much as you can when you aren't taking care of your own work [*or job*], or, if you're not employed, then volunteering to help meet these needs. When hard work is going on to meet these simple, basic needs, all other good will follow because, in struggling first-hand against this tangible evil [*need*], you'll discover the real nature of *all* evil. As you come up against various kinds of resistance, you'll figure out where the real fault lies and who the real enemy of good is. You'll also discover help in the most unexpected places. You'll learn profound lessons and discern truths that detached speculation could never have revealed. As soon as you make an effort to do something, you'll find that the problem of education is solved because everybody will ferret out their own best way to be of use, and will find a way to learn whatever they need to know. Competive exams will finally be useful because they'll be happening naturally every day on the field while working. As the work is done, small, practical arts and skills will be enhanced by greater arts and theoretical sciences. [*Art and research will no longer be merely theoretical amusements, but will have immediate practical application that will spur artists and researchers on to further work.*]

But that's not all. On this honest and basic work, we will finally find an infallible religion. The greatest and most terrible of all of life's mysteries is how even the most sincere religion is corrupted when it's not daily based on reasonable, effective, humble and helpful *action*. Notice that I said *helpful* action. There is one principle that, when followed, keeps all religions pure, but when disobeyed, makes all religions false. No matter what religious faith, whether dark or enlightened, if we allow ourselves to dwell on the issues we disagree on, then we're wrong and under satan's power. That's what the Pharisee was doing when they prayed, 'Lord, I thank you that I am not as other men are.' At every moment of our lives, we should be trying to find out, not where other people differ from us, but where we are in agreement. The moment we find something kind or good we can agree on to do (and surely we can find something), we should do it. We should work at it together. It's hard for two people to quarrel when they're exerting themselves side by side. But as soon as even the best men stop pushing and start talking, they start to mistake dogma for righteousness, and then it's all over. I won't even bring up the crimes that have been committed in the name of Christ, or the mistakes that people think are consistent with and obedient to God's will. But I will bring up the deadly corruption and waste of essential strength in religious emotion, when the pure strength of God's truth that should be the guiding light of every nation and the splendor and purity of every youth is rejected. You see girls all the time who have never thoroughly learned to do a single useful thing. They can't cook, can't sew, can't balance a checkbook, can't prepare treatments for illnesses. Their entire lives have been spent either in playing or in pride. When girls like these have earnest hearts, they take their inborn religious passion that was supposed to support them through the mundane duties of daily life, and instead waste it on anxious, useless dwelling over the meaning of difficult passages in the Bible that were never intended to be understood by thinking, but only by doing. All of the instinctive wisdom and mercy of womanhood is made dysfunctional, and their pure consciences warped into futile agony over some question that a life of serving would have solved in an instant, or else kept them too busy to think about. A girl like this should have real, meaningful work that will keep her active in the morning and tired at night, with the knowledge that others will be better off because of what she did during that day. Then her enthusiasm will not be misspent on worrying, but will transform itself into a majestic, radiant and kind-hearted peace.

It's similar with our students. We used to teach them to conjugate Latin verbs and then call them educated. These days, we graduate them with athletic scholarships and call them educated. But can they plow a field? Can they sow and plant at the right time? Can they construct a sturdy structure? They spend their lives trying to be pure, noble, faithful, fair-minded, saying and doing what is right. Some of these youths carry the strength and hope of our country within them. But we have to turn their courage from the work of war, and turn it to the work of mercy. We have to turn their intellects from debating about words to identifying priorities. We have to turn their desire for adventure away from fighting for country, and turn it towards being loyal to a true kingly power. Then there will finally be a contentment that never dies, and a religion that's correct. Faith will no longer be attacked by temptation or defended by violence and fear. Hope will no longer be extinguished by long, overwelming years, or disgraced by betraying lies. Hope will abide with us, and not only hope, but something even greater: the will of God [*to love*], and the name and nature of God [*God is Love*] will also abide with us. 'For the greatest of these is Love.'

ABOUT THE AUTHORS

John Ruskin (1819-1900) was an art critic and champion of the artist J.M.W. Turner as well as Pre-Raphaelite art. He was also an artist in his own right.

Leslie Noelani Laurio is one of the original Advisory/creators of the AmblesideOnline homeschool curriculum for which this book was paraphrased. She has also paraphrased the six volumes of Charlotte Mason's books on education.

Made in the USA
Columbia, SC
04 January 2018